Tulika

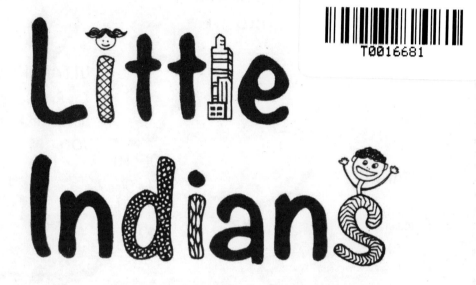

Little Indians

Stories from across the country

 by Pika Nani

design and illustrations **Shreya Mehta**

CONTENTS

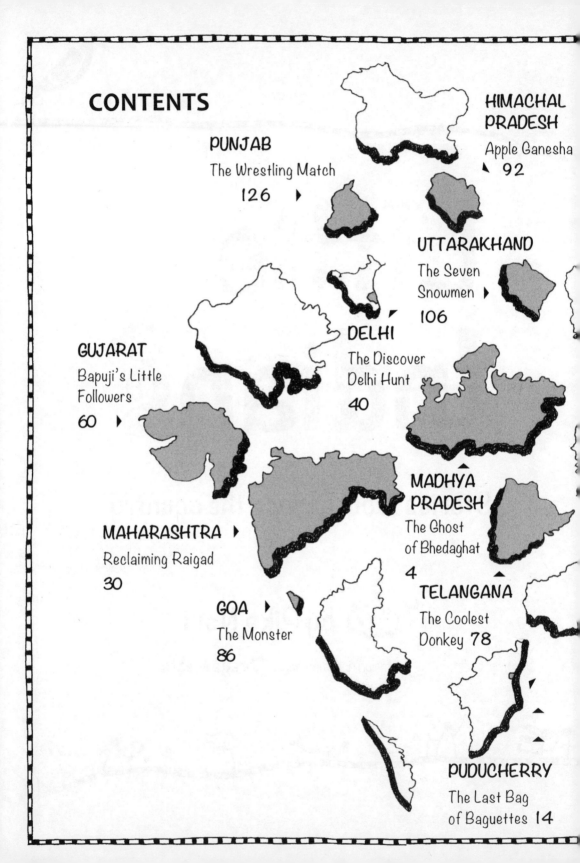

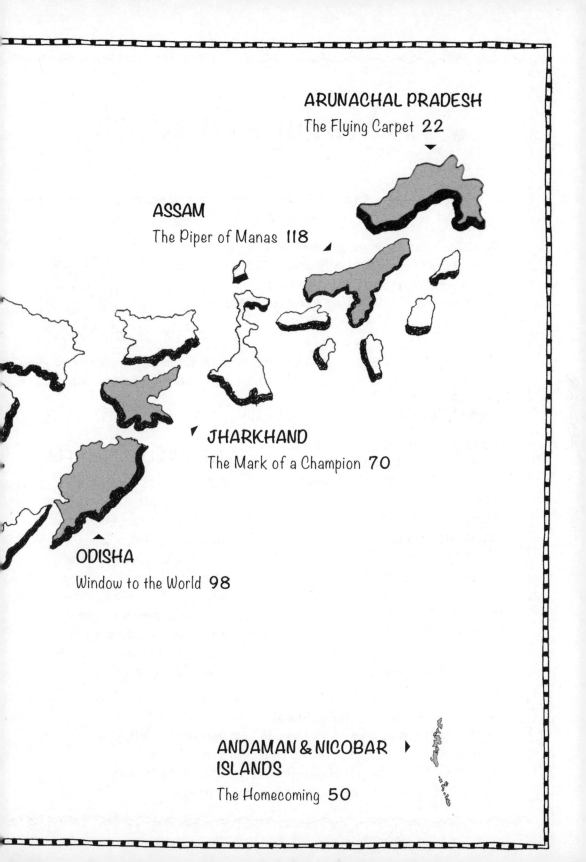

Madhya Pradesh

── Where in Madhya Pradesh did Rudyard Kipling set The Jungle Book? ──

Pench Tiger Reserve in the Satpura Hills. Many of the locations really exist — the Wainganga River with its gorge where Shere Khan was killed, Kanhiwara village and the Seoni ('Seeonee') Hills.

MP is Tigerland! Most of India's tigers live in the state's forest reserves such as Kanha, Bandhavgarh, Pench, Panna and Satpura.

◀◀ REWIND

One of the earliest kingdoms here was Avanti (6th century BCE), roughly today's Malwa. Most major dynasties of India ruled in this region — the Mauryans, Guptas, Mughals, Marathas and finally the British.

Madhya Pradesh............

Chattisgarh............

THE EARLIEST PEOPLE

Different tribal groups or Adivasis live all over MP, mainly the Gond, Bhil, Baiga, Korku, Bhariya, Halba, Kaul, Mariya, and Sahariya, with sub-tribes and others. Each group has its own language, lifestyle and culture. But they all believe in animism, the worship of nature, and have also borrowed from Christianity, Islam, Jainism and Hinduism.

In 1947, two new states, Madhya Bharat and Vindhya Pradesh, were created here. VP was then joined to MB along with Bhopal (till then a princely state) and a new MP was formed in 1956, the largest state in India. It turned out to be too large. So in 2000, part of it was broken off to make Chhattisgarh.

WAVY WEAVES

Maheshwar has an old tradition of handweaving beautiful fabrics, especially the Maheshwari sari. Delicate, wave-like patterns on the sari borders seem to capture the ripples of the Narmada that flows by. The weaves from another town, Chanderi, are so fine, soft and transparent that they are referred to as 'woven air'.

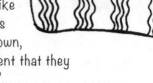

ROCK ART

The Bhimbetka caves near Bhopal have stunning rock paintings that go back over 10,000 years, to the Stone Age!

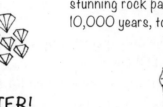

GLITTER!

Mineral-rich Madhya Pradesh has the largest reserves of diamond and copper in India. Panna is the only producer of diamonds in the country. But there is a lot of illegal mining, so despite its diamonds, Panna is one of the poorest districts.

I COME FROM MP

Tansen, the father of Hindustani classical music was one of the nine jewels of Akbar's court. It is said he could bring down rain by singing Raga Megh Malhar and light up a fire with Raga Deepak!

The legacy continued. Sarod maestro Ustad Amjad Ali Khan, vocalist Kumar Gandharva, and playback singers Lata Mangeshkar and Kishore Kumar were all born in MP. So too was freedom fighter Chandra Shekhar Azad.

the Ghost of Bhedaghat

It was an enchanted night at Bhedaghat. The Narmada gurgled gently through a gorge with towering marble rocks on both sides. The full moon played hide and seek with the clouds. One moment the valley was plunged into darkness, and the next the moonlight was making magic. It cast its spell on the river and made it look like the Milky Way. It cast its spell also on the white rocks and they glittered and shone like pieces of the moon.

But its magic had no effect on the only spectator present — a lean, dark skinned boy of about 12, named Dheeraj.

It could have been because something was worrying him. Or it could have been because he had already made about ten trips that night in his rowboat, ferrying tourists through the Valley of Marbles, giving them the usual lyrical commentary (which the tourists loved!) about the beauty of Bhedaghat.

"Bhedaghat dekhna chandni raat mein, camera haath mein, family saath mein. See Bhedaghat on moonlit nights, camera in your hand, family by your side!" he would gush dramatically in Hindi. Pointing out to rocks shaped like a car, a bull, a face, he'd say, "Look at the natural modern art — yahi toh hai Bhedaghat, this is Bhedaghat!"

Now it was well past midnight and the place was deserted. The shutters were down, the floodlights were switched off. But the show was not over.

Dheeraj had decided to spend the night at his mother's little souvenir shop on the ghat, but he had not been able to sleep. He sat on the steps leading to the jetty where the boats were moored, wrapped in his shawl, and lost in his thoughts.

Suddenly he was alerted by the sound of approaching footsteps. On an impulse, he hid behind the side wall and peered out.

Three men were hurrying towards the river. Just then, the moon partially emerged from the clouds and Dheeraj could see their faces.

He recognised the person in the middle — a tall, thin man with a balding head of silver hair, wearing thick, round spectacles. They got into a boat and were soon out of sight.

Dheeraj waited for a few minutes, dashed to his own boat and began to row after them.

Who were the men with Prof. Tripathi? Where was the professor going so late at night? Maybe . . . just maybe . . . he had finally found the treasure!

It had all started just three weeks ago. An old man, wearing a waterproof jacket and a sun hat, and carrying a bulging backpack, had come for a ride on Dheeraj's boat. Initially Dheeraj had thought he was just another tourist out to explore the famous Marble Rocks of Bhedaghat, a small town near the city of Jabalpur in Madhya Pradesh.

But the old man, who introduced himself as Professor Gaurishankar Tripathi from Delhi, was not an ordinary tourist.

His behaviour was most extraordinary.

He would look through his binoculars and ask Dheeraj to stop abruptly near some cliffs. He took photographs of the white stones from different angles and carefully collected tiny particles of the rocks with a brush and a dustpan. He would keep scribbling something in his diary and his backpack was full of strange equipment.

Every day, the professor would spend a few hours on the river, and had hired Dheeraj's boat exclusively for a month. Though he was curious, Dheeraj kept quiet as he did not wish to lose his customer. Prof. Tripathi seldom talked, but sometimes he asked questions, which Dheeraj readily answered.

One day, in his usual abrupt style, the professor asked Dheeraj: "Do you know who I am?"

Not waiting for a reply, he continued.

"I am a professor of archaeology. Do you know what that means?"

"Ar-chae-o-what? Pata nahi, saab. I don't know."

"Archaeology is the scientific study of human culture and behaviour, through the recovery, documentation and analysis of material remains," said the professor, who was used to mouthing the definition in his classes.

"To put it simply, an archaeologist is someone who studies people and what they did in the past from the things they left behind."

This time Dheeraj understood and seemed suitably impressed.

Prof. Tripathi then looked around in a sinister manner and lowered his voice. "This is highly confidential. I was in Mandu Fort doing some research when I stumbled upon something big. I found a secret document, a sort of parchment . . . an old letter. According to it, when invaders were about to attack the fort, the king gave a secret order to hide the royal treasures in different parts of his kingdom. The letter says that a big diamond, second only to the Kohinoor, was hidden amongst the rocks of Bhedaghat. All the other treasures were later retrieved, but the one hidden here was never found!"

"What a great story! But do you really think it is true?"

"Of course it is true! I have studied the document in detail. It is authentic. And if such a big diamond had been found, we would have known by now. I am convinced the diamond is still here!"

"I see! And you are here to look for it," said Dheeraj trying to mask his excitement. "But why are you telling me all this?"

"You are an honest and sincere boy. You have never tried to cheat me of my money. I keep forgetting my things in your boat, but you always return them. I know I can trust you. Fact is, I need someone to help me. I have searched the lower parts of the marble valley from the boat. I need someone to climb onto the cliffs and search the tops of the rocks. If we find the diamond, you will also be famous and will be rewarded."

"When do we start?" was all Dheeraj could manage to say.

For the next five days, Dheeraj put all his efforts into helping the professor. He climbed onto the rocks, took photographs and collected samples. They had gone as far as Bandar Kudni, the narrowest point of the gorge, where Hanuman is believed to have set foot on his way to Lanka.

The previous morning, the old man had made him climb a steep cliff, the top of which resembled a wolf's head. There was a deep cut in the rock, forming the wolf's mouth. Dheeraj had felt a thrill as he had put his hand inside. But there were just the remains of a bird's nest. What a letdown!

Even Prof. Tripathi seemed disappointed. He said he needed to analyse the document further, and would not come the next day. Dropping him off at the jetty, Dheeraj had called out, "Tomorrow is full moon night. At least come in the evening, I have something special to show you."

"Of course! I will be there," the professor had replied.

Dheeraj had waited all evening for the professor to arrive. But he had not turned up — until now.

The sight of the boat brought Dheeraj back to the present. It had stopped a few metres ahead. Thankfully, the valley had been quite dark all through the chase. He moved closer to the cliffs and stayed in the shadows. On the opposite side was a small nook where he could hide his boat, and he rowed there silently.

"They must be here for the treasure. He is trying to cheat me of my reward," thought Dheeraj, his face burning with anger.

The next moment, he was frozen to the spot.

The moon had just emerged from the clouds and he could see the three men standing on top of a cliff. A burly man had a knife pointed at the professor, whose hands were tied. The other man had a long spear, in his hand. He could hear their voices echo.

"Okay, this is your last chance. Tell us where the treasure is. Quickly, or else . . ." the man with the knife was saying.

"I don't know. I'm telling you I don't know! Please don't hurt me," the professor pleaded.

"Don't try to fool us! We overheard you talking about a hidden treasure and have been following you for two days," said the other man, in a nasal voice.

Dheeraj's heart was beating loudly. He knew he had to save the professor. But if he went back for help, it would be too late. He didn't have much time. He had to act fast.

He looked up. He was below a cliff directly opposite them. An idea was already forming in his mind. But would it work? Both his and the professor's lives depended on it!

Dheeraj put a few things in a bag and started carefully climbing the cliff. It was the same one they had come to yesterday. On reaching the top, he set to work. He camouflaged himself in his shawl and, just like the previous day, he crawled on his stomach and reached the edge of the cliff.

Luckily, it was dark again. He slid his hand down the wolf-shaped rock, put a torch in the mouth and switched it on. The wolf's face was lit

up by an eerie greenish blue light. The strong beam shone straight on the kidnappers, blinding them for an instant, giving Dheeraj enough time to crawl behind a boulder.

"AWOOOoooooo, AWooooooooo!" howled Dheeraj into a hollow tin can. The voice echoed loudly.

"Who is there?" shouted the goons, taken aback.

"I AM THE GHOST OF BHEDAGHAT," Dheeraj announced.

"Th ... th ... there is no such thing as ghosts," stammered the man with the nasal voice.

"You fool! Every year, on the full moon night of this month, I come to guard my valley. If you cause any trouble I will destroy you. AWoooooooOOOO ...."

The kidnappers looked shocked but didn't move.

Dheeraj knew he had to do something drastic to convince them. He prayed they would fall for his trick.

The moon was tired of playing games and was still resting behind a dark cloud.

Dheeraj now had the advantage of seeing them, while they couldn't see him. He moved towards the wolf's head and lit a match.

"Enough! You have made me really angry. Now you will suffer!" his voice boomed.

Zooooom! Two streaks of fire whizzed ahead right above the kidnapper's heads, like burning arrows from the wolf's eyes.

The two men dropped their weapons and bolted for their lives. Dheeraj heard the thud as they landed on their boat.

He came out of his hiding spot only when their boat was out of sight.

Professor Tripathi! He still had to rescue him!

Dheeraj climbed down and rowed towards him. He bounded up the cliff and found the old man sitting in a daze.

"Professor saab! It was me. I hope I didn't scare you," he said untying the old man's hands.

"Dheeraj, my boy, I knew you had come to save me!"

"You did? You recognised your torch then!"

"Yes. But tell me, the streak of fire ... What was it?"

"Firecrackers! They were firecrackers! Remember, I told you I had something special for you? I was going to light those rockets from the banks. It would reflect in the water and on the rocks. The effect would be spectacular!"

"Ah! The effect it had on those kidnappers has been spectacular enough for me!" said Prof. Tripathi, and they both laughed.

"But seriously, you are so brave ... you risked your life for me. I ... I don't know how to thank you ..." the professor went on with feeling.

"Let's get back first. You can thank me later," replied Dheeraj, a little embarrassed.

The next day, when Prof. Tripathi went to the police station, he found the kidnappers already in the lock-up. A constable on beat had found the men the previous night, scrambling up the steps of the ghat ranting about a ghost.

He had recognised the duo as wanted criminals, and taken them into custody immediately.

Shaken by the incident, the professor decided to give up his search and return to Delhi. "Let Bhedaghat keep its secrets," he told Dheeraj. "Anyway, our efforts will not be completely wasted. We have collected so much information about this place that I am planning to write a book. *Bhedaghat, the Valley of Diamonds*, I shall call it. And by diamonds I will now mean the glittering white marble rocks — they too are a treasure!"

Dheeraj was not too upset about giving up the search for the diamond. After all, he had been bestowed with a bravery award and the professor had got him a scholarship to a good school in Jabalpur.

With Prof. Tripathi's help, Dheeraj and his mother moved to the city and led a comfortable life.

Back at Bhedaghat, the boatmen included another verse to their commentary. Pointing to the wolf-shaped rock they would proclaim:

"A boy, clever and brave at heart,
Fought villains alone, by being smart,
And turned this rock into
The ghost of Bhedaghat!"

DIGGING UP THE PAST

Thanks to archaeologists who go digging and looking for clues to discover the past, we now know a great deal more about Madhya Pradesh. From pre-historic rock shelters, rock-cut caves, stupas, viharas, temples and forts, there are interesting pointers to people long ago and how they lived. Of these, Bhimbetka and Sanchi are the most unique.

In 1957, Indian archaeologist Dr Vishnu Wakankar discovered the rock shelters of Bhimbetka quite by accident. There are 750 of them, out of which 500 have rock paintings that go as far back as from the Mesolithic age (roughly 10,000–6000 BCE) to the Early Medieval age (8th–13th century CE). Done in different styles, and mainly in red and white, the scenes depict stick figures of humans, animals, and everyday events like hunting, dancing and more.

On a hill sits the village of Sanchi, the oldest Buddhist site in existence. After the 13th century CE it was almost forgotten until General Taylor, a British officer, discovered it in 1818, half buried, yet well preserved.

The Great Stupa, one of India's oldest stone structures, constructed by Emperor Ashoka, is on every pilgrim's must-visit list. It was built to shelter relics related to Buddha and its architecture is meant to reflect honour and respect for him.

Puducherry

BORN APART

Yanam............

Puducherry must be the only Union Territory of India to be so scattered! This is because it is made of four former French colonies, now its four districts, which are physically unconnected. Puducherry (the biggest, with the capital city) and Karaikal are in Tamil Nadu, Yanam is much further north in Andhra Pradesh, and Mahe is in Kerala. The first three are on the Bay of Bengal, and the fourth is across the country, on the Arabian Sea. Tamil, Telugu, Malayalam and French are all official languages in this small UT!

............Mahe

Puducherry ....
Karaikal.................

REWIND

Puducherry has a long history of maritime trade with Europe. The Romans came as far back as the 1st century CE.

The Portuguese, the Danes, the Dutch, the French and the English have all been here and fought many battles over this area.

But it was the French who left behind a lasting influence, most visible in the city of Puducherry. They first came there in 1673 and transformed the little fishing village — then called Puducheri, meaning 'new settlement' — into a rich port town. After shuttling frequently between the English and the French, it finally came under French control from 1816.

It was handed over to Independent India in 1954 but remained a French possession. It was only in 1963 that the French parliament finally ratified it as part of India.

Puducheri became Pondicherry under the French. In 2006 the name officially changed to Puducherry. But for most, it is still simply Pondy!

I COME FROM PUDUCHERRY

Aurobindo Ghosh was a Bengali scholar, poet, and nationalist turned philosopher. Born in Calcutta, he had a very English education in London and Cambridge. But back in India, he joined the anti-British movement. He then moved to Pondicherry and spent the rest of his life in the study of philosophy and yoga. He founded the Sri Aurobindo Ashram.

Tamil poet Bharathidasan was actually Kanaga Subburathinam, but he preferred to call himself after the great poet Subramania Bharathiar.

WHICH CAME FIRST?

Some say Mahe was named after Bertrand François Mahé de La Bourdonnais, a French officer. Others say that the local Malayalam name for the place was, and still is, Mayyazhi, meaning 'eyebrow of the sea'. The French possibly shortenened it to Mayye, then Mahe, and La Bourdonnais made it part of his name. Who knows!

RAGS TO BAGS

At a paper factory in Puducherry city, cotton rags are pulped, dyed and pressed to make strong sheets of paper. Straw, flower petals, coir, banana bark . . . almost anything is added for texture! This is used to make bags, boxes, books and a lot else.

HOLLYWOOD CALLING!

Puducherry's Western connection goes further than its colonial past — all the way to Hollywood! Indian-American filmmaker Manoj Night Shyamalan, who made The Sixth Sense, Unbreakable, Signs, After Earth and others, is from Mahe.

And the Oscar winning film Life of Pi was shot partly in Puducherry city, for that's where Pi grew up. The Botanical Gardens turned into his family's zoo, the pier was the setting for Pi's farewell scene with his teenage love, and the French Quarter a backdrop for the film's first scenes.

LIFE OF PI

The Last Bag of Baguettes

It was at the break of dawn on a fine Saturday morning that young Carthic Manickme and his father made their way to their small bakery down Rue Victor Simonel.

Rue? Isn't that French for street? So is this the Pondicherry of 200 years ago, when it was a thriving French colony?

Oh no! This is a recent story. Pondicherry is now Puducherry but the French Quarter, the area where Carthic's father had a bakery, is still very French — the buildings, the street names, the French-ish spellings of Indian names . . . And that's also where you get the long French bread, the baguette.

The Manickme family had run their little shop, Bakers & Sons, for generations, baking fresh handmade baguettes every morning. They still followed the original recipe that had been handed down by Carthic's great-great grandfather, who had learnt it from a French cook. Since then Bakers & Sons had flourished and, at its peak, had customers queuing up for the golden brown loaf that was crusty on the outside, deliciously chewy inside.

The shop had always managed to survive amidst growing competition from other bakeries and other types of breads. But in the last six months, business had come spiralling down with the opening of Hotel Le Paris down the street, which had a chic café that also sold bakery products.

At first, Bala Manickme, Carthic's father, had thought the hype would wear off and his customers would be back as usual. But after six months all his savings had been depleted, his assistants had left, and just a handful of his customers remained.

Bala had finally reached a decision to close down his bakery and had told his son about it the night before.

Carthic had been appalled. "But why, Appa? We make the best baguettes in town!"

"We do! But times have changed. It is what they say . . . it's all about the marketing. I cannot afford to advertise in newspapers and TV, like Le Paris. I cannot fit fancy furniture and TV screens in our old bakery. Nobody cares for genuine taste anymore," Bala had reasoned. "I am afraid we have no other option."

And so, this Saturday morning, Bakers & Sons opened its doors for the last time.

Bala had just enough ingredients left to bake one last batch of six, and wanted his son to have them. He knew how much Carthic would miss their baguettes.

He worked the dough, resting it in between for it to rise. Then he shaped six long, log-like baguettes, making three slashes on top of each. They went into the ancient oven that was still fired with wood and dry leaves.

Soon the warm aroma of freshly baked bread filled the bakery. Putting the baguettes into the trademark brown paper bag with 'Bakers & Sons' proudly printed on it, Bala presented them to his son.

Carthic held the bag in his hands. He wanted to say something, but couldn't. In a few moments they both might have cried, but that was averted by the sudden appearance of an old woman asking for baguettes.

"Sorry, amma, we don't have any more," said Bala, trying to sound casual.

"I have walked so far to come to your bakery," said the old woman. "Don't you have any left? What about this bag here?" She pointed to the bag Carthic was holding.

"That is our very last bag of baguettes. I baked these especially for my son!" burst out Bala, unable to control his emotions.

"It's okay, Appa. One baguette is all I need." Saying this, Carthic took one baguette out and handed over the paper bag to the old woman.

Venkamma was pleased by the young boy's gesture. However, she did not really understand the true significance of Carthic's sacrifice. She merely thought it was the last bag of baguettes for the day. But she blessed him and started walking home.

Although well into her sixties and with many broken teeth, Venkamma was still as fond of baguettes as she had been when a young

girl. She now ate them softened in sweetened coconut milk that had been flavoured with cardamom.

Walking along Bharathi Park, she went past the Vinayagar temple and reached the crossing near the serene Sri Aurobindo Ashram. It was still early in the morning, but there were quite a few bikers cycling past. Just then, a man clad in a white shirt and white veshti approached her. Venkamma guessed he was from the ashram. He took her arm and offered to help her across the road. Grateful, Venkamma took one baguette and gave him the brown bag, saying, "One baguette is all I need."

Hébert was too surprised and touched to refuse. He worked in the ashram library, a few blocks away from the main ashram complex. He had come to India from France as a backpacker and travelled widely, before finding his home in Puducherry and his calling at the Aurobindo Ashram. Hébert had skipped breakfast that morning as he was getting late, but had not thought twice about stopping to help the old lady. "It must be divine will that I shouldn't go hungry!" he smiled, as he walked down Rue de la Marine. He could eat a baguette with his coffee at the library.

"Stop! STOP!" a voice called out, making Hébert stop short and turn around. A schoolboy with a football in one hand was close on his heels and pointing to something. Hébert's gaze went down and he saw that he had just been saved from stepping into a dirty puddle which would have soiled his white clothes.

"Thank you!" said Hébert. Reaching into the bag of baguettes, he took one out and gave the bag with the rest to the boy. "One baguette is all I need," he smiled.

Arul was returning from an early morning football practice match, in which he had scored two winning goals. Shoving the bag into his rucksack he continued down the street, dribbling his football and replaying the match in his mind. He had reached Goubert Avenue, better known as Beach Road, when the football slipped out of his hands and rolled onto the wide street.

Arul was about to run behind it when he saw, to his horror, a truck and a car speeding down the road. He stepped back and closed his eyes, certain that his precious football would come under the wheels of one of them and burst.

But a shrill whistle stopped both the vehicles just in time. A tall policeman had already picked up the ball and was coming towards Arul.

"Paathu, thambi — careful, my boy! A main road like this is not for practising football. You could have had an accident," he said, handing the ball back. Arul went red in the face and nodded. Then, suddenly remembering, he pulled out the brown bag from his rucksack. "One baguette is all I need!" he grinned, pulling out one and putting the bag in the policeman's hands. He hurried off biting into his baguette.

Doraiswamy was pleased. He had just an hour to go before finishing his morning beat, and hoped his wife had made some good, spicy mutton curry which he could have with the baguette. He continued his walk along the seaside promenade and reached the Gandhi statue. The glistening sea crashed on the rocks and the narrow strip of beach stretched endlessly. The place was calm and quiet now, but by evening it would be crowded with revellers and tourists.

Holding his baton and the bag in one hand, Doraiswamy was straightening the red French-style kepi on his head when, suddenly, a strong gust of wind whisked it away. He ran after it, but a little girl on a bicycle had already caught it.

"Thank you, thank you, ma!" said Doraiswamy, replacing the cap firmly on his head. "Hope you can ride that cycle well, ma. There is a lot of traffic this morning!" he added in a policeman's tone.

"My house is nearby, Sir. I am going there now."

Doraiswamy softened and put the bag of baguettes — minus one — in her cycle basket. "One baguette is all I need," he told her.

Jennine thanked the policeman shyly, and pedalled off. She had gone cycling with her friends early that morning in the quiet by-lanes of the French Quarter. The others had turned back near the Dupleix statue. Only Jennine had continued down the road enjoying the sea breeze, till a red policeman's cap slapped into her face and almost knocked her off her cycle.

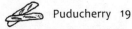

She now took a turn near the Town Hall and soon reached a restored French villa, painted a bright sunshine yellow with white bands around the doors and windows. It had louvered shutters and a long wooden balcony held up by iron brackets. She hurried in through the back door hoping she'd made it before breakfast time, for she hadn't told her father she was going out.

The breakfast table was set but, thankfully, her father had not yet come down. Jennine suddenly remembered the paper bag the policeman had given her, and went out to get it. In it was a single baguette. She cut it lengthwise in half. On one long piece she placed tomato slices, drizzled olive oil and garnished it with cheese and basil leaves. She was about to bite into it when her father joined her at the table.

Jennine offered her slice to her father, but he took the plain half and bit into it. The thin, glazed crust had the perfect crunch and the centre was light and chewy. "Hmm! This is a perfectly baked baguette if I have ever seen one," he said. "But I don't remember bringing home any."

"Yummm! This is the best I've ever tasted!" said Jennine quickly, trying to stop the question on her father's mind.

Paul Dubois frowned and was about to continue, when he saw the brown paper bag with Bakers & Sons printed on it. He picked it up and turned to his daughter. "So, where did this come from?"

He let his daughter off with a warning to never again go anywhere without telling him. Then he finished his breakfast and set off with the paper bag in hand.

Bala and Carthic had tidied up the bakery, cleaned the counters and the stove, and packed the equipment. They had worked silently, each putting up a brave front for the other's sake. Bala was just downing the shutters, when they saw a man walking towards their shop.

"Excuse me, do you make the baguettes that come in this bag," Paul asked Bala, holding out the paper bag.

"Yes. But sorry, we are out of baguettes, so please try some other place."

"How about tomorrow?"

"We are not opening tomorrow or any other day for that matter! Bakers & Sons is closed forever!" said Bala irritably.

"Really? What a shame! My name is Paul Dubois and I own Hotel Le Paris down the road. It has a fine café, but my chef makes terrible baguettes. I was hoping you would supply them to us from now on. Yours are … parfaites … perfect!"

Different emotions ran across Bala's face as he stood listening to the man who was his biggest competitor, who had forced him to close shop, and who was now proposing to be his best ally! Bala was speechless. He looked at Carthic who nodded happily at him.

"You've got a deal!" said Bala to Paul.

"But the baguettes will be sold under the name of Bakers & Sons," Carthic added quickly.

"Agreed!" said Paul, holding out his hand.

"How many would you need?" asked Bala, shaking hands warmly.

"A few hundreds every morning is all we need!" replied Paul.

BAGUETTES AND BAKERIES

It's hard on the outside. Really hard. But Pondy locals have found their own ways to soften this long French bread while eating — some with thick coconut milk sweetened with sugar and flavoured with cardamom, others with spicy mutton curry. By breakfast time, most of the 30 or so bakeries have piles of baguettes waiting to fly off the shelves. One particular bakery sells around 300-400 of them every day!

Arunachal Pradesh

If you are a late riser, Dong isn't for you — at the easternmost point of India, this village has the earliest sunrise! But if you're up anyway, take a walk along the left bank of the Lohit river (that later becomes Brahmaputra) on which Dong stands, for stupendous views of pine forests and snow-capped mountains.

DRIVING HIGH

78 km from Tawang is the Sela Pass. At around 14,000 ft, it is the world's second highest motorable pass, connecting Tawang with the rest of India.

Arunachal has independent countries on three sides — Bhutan on its west, Myanmar on the east, and the Tibet region of China to the north.

14,000 ft

◀◀ REWIND

Historical details about this area are sketchy. What little is known is from oral history and some ruins. There are many, many tribal groups — Nyishi, Monpa, Miri, Tagin, Apatani, Adi, Mishmi, Khamti and more — each with its own distinct culture and religious beliefs. Some of them took to agriculture quite early, and others excelled in handicrafts.

The British occupied this area after the Anglo-Burmese War (1824-26). They called it the North East Frontier Agency (NEFA), and it was part of Assam.

It became a Union Territory in 1972 and was named Arunachal Pradesh.

BIO-RICH! Over 5000 species of plants, about 85 land mammals, over 500 birds and different kinds of butterflies, insects and reptiles. What makes Arunachal so rich? It lies at the junction of the Paleoarctic, Indo-Chinese, and Indo-Malayan bio-geographic regions, which ensures that creatures from all these regions are found here.

MONASTERY IN THE MIST

Dragon gates, unspoiled lakes, waterfalls, brooks and streams... The Tawang region up in the eastern Himalayas is home mainly to the Buddhist Monpa and Sherdukpen tribes. The centuries old Tawang Monastery here is the largest Buddhist monastery in India and the biggest in Asia outside Lhasa, Tibet. Its painted wooden windows, religious motifs and prayer flags are all very Tibetan. It has residential quarters for monks, a three-storied library, and a Buddhist cultural centre.

A DOSE OF REBE

Rebe (Begonia tessaricarpa), a rare medicinal plant, was believed to be extinct. Last seen in 1890, it was found after 115 years in 2005 in the Upper Subansiri district. The local Adi and Tagin tribes use it to treat stomach ache and dehydration.

CAT PARK

Namdapha National Park is the only sanctuary in India where four major varieties of the big cats — tiger, leopard, clouded leopard and snow leopard — are found. The red panda and the highly endangered white winged wood duck also live here.

HANDS ON

The locals craft elegant furniture, baskets, bags, hats and even jewellery in cane and bamboo. They also make beautiful masks which are used in dances and pantomimes held during religious and festive occasions.

— What's in a name? —

What is common to the three do tell, Foxtail, Lady-slipper and Jewel?

Ans: All three are orchids. Arunachal has around 600 species, and Asia's third largest orchidarium is at Tipi.

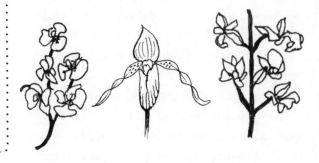

The Flying Carpet

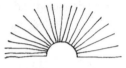

In the easternmost tip of India, where the sun first rises, is Arunachal Pradesh, and there in the cradle of the Himalayas lies Tawang. It is a valley overflowing with nature's abundance, home to ancient tribes, and named after the 400-year-old Tawang Monastery. This is a paradise hidden, unexplored, and in the limelight only rarely, as during a visit by the Dalai Lama.

In one of the time-forgotten villages of Tawang lived a little girl called Sibsa, with her mother Sangey. Sibsa was five years old. She had red chubby cheeks, straight shoulder length hair and a fringe that covered most of her forehead.

Mother and daughter lived in a small hut made of stones and wooden planks. A shed adjoining the house served as a workshop. Like most women of the Monpa tribe, who are the main inhabitants of Tawang, Sangey was a skilled weaver. Besides weaving their traditional clothes she made hand-knotted carpets and sold them to showrooms in Tawang city. Sibsa's father lived far away, in Mumbai, working in a cane furniture shop. He had moved there with the hope of making more money to give his family a better life, especially a good education to Sibsa.

One day, Sibsa came home from school full of excitement. Her teacher had read out a story about a prince and his flying carpet and she couldn't wait to tell it to her mother.

Sibsa found her sitting in front of the loom in their workshop. Sangey was wearing a long red and white striped dress and a woollen jacket, the cloth for both of which she had woven herself.

"Zi tshai du lo? What are you doing?" asked Sibsa, settling down next to her.

"I was just getting started on my next carpet. How was school?"

"Good! Our teacher told us a great story today." Sibsa repeated the story, complete with actions. "Wouldn't it be great if we had a carpet like that?" she said at the end, a little out of breath.

"Yes, my little one, it would be wonderful."

"You will make it then?"

"What?"

"A flying carpet! I can fly everywhere on it."

Sangey remembered how her little girl had wanted to grow wings so she could fly like birds and how, recently, she had been fascinated by the aeroplanes that occasionally flew over Tawang. And now, this!

"So, Ma, will you make one for me? You make such beautiful carpets," said Sibsa, in her sweetest voice.

Her mother smiled. "Oh, but carpets can't really fly, Sibsa dear!"

"But it does in the story! Our teacher said so!"

Sangey knew that for Sibsa, what her teacher said was the final word. So she tried another approach, "The carpet in the story was magical, but I don't know any magic."

"But Ma, I remember Daddy saying that your hands create magic on the loom!"

"Not the kind of magic to make carpets fly, you silly girl!" laughed her mother.

Tears welled up in Sibsa's eyes and trickled down her cheeks. All her dreams of flying had come crashing down.

"I am sorry. I didn't mean to make fun of you, Sibsa. Don't be so sad," said Sangey, kissing away the tears. "Okay, I will try to make a magic carpet for you if you promise to be a good girl and not disturb me while I work."

Sibsa's face brightened up and she gave her mother a tight hug.

Sibsa waited patiently for the next 20 days for the carpet to be finished. She watched her mother working on the upright wooden frame, looping the colourful woollen threads and knotting the carpet with deft motions of her hands. She kept her promise and did not go to the workshop, except when Sangey called for her to help with fetching wool or cutting the threads.

Finally, the carpet was ready.

Sangey spread it on an old wooden table at the back of the workshop. The carpet was inky-blue. It had a majestic mountain in the centre with snowy peaks, clusters of moss-green trees and the golden roof of a gonpa, a Buddhist monastery, rising above the treetops. Brown huts dotted the slopes and an icy lake rested at the bottom. On both sides of the mountain were large butterfly shaped, yellow-maroon and pink-purple orchids. Criss-cross patterns formed the border, with a dancing

yak at each corner. It was like a 3x5 ft portrait of Tawang. Simply stunning!

Sangey made Sibsa wipe her hands and feet and then lifted her up and placed her on the carpet.

"This is the most beautiful thing ever!" cried Sibsa "Now how do I make it fly?"

"You have to just use your imagination."

"Im-ma-gition? I don't think I have it. Can I use my hands instead?"

Sibsa tried to push the carpet with her hands, and the table wobbled and creaked.

"Not like that!" said her mother, stopping her. "Of course you have imagination. Like when you play with your doll–"

"But Ma, I want to FLY, not play," Sibsa cut her short.

"Yes, my little one. With imagination you can go where you want to go, see what you want to see and be who you want to be," said Sangey, sitting on the table behind her daughter.

"Come, let me show you. Hold tight, we are taking off!" She leaned back, pulling Sibsa with her. "We are zooming out of the door . . . flying higher and higher . . . we are up in the sky now . . ."

She pointed to a small square hut on the carpet, "Look, our house seems so tiny from here … Hey! Watch out for that tree!" and they swivelled to the right.

"Ma, that's not a tree," giggled Sibsa. "It's a flagpost of the gonpa!"

"See, you are better than me at imagining," said Sangey, and they both had a hearty laugh.

Sibsa was very happy with her flying carpet. Her imagination soared with the carpet and took her to a different place every day.

She flew over gonpas, zigzagging through prayer flags fluttering in the wind. She flew over mountains and gave grazing yaks a fright. She flew low over the lakes and splashed the cool waters with her hand.

She went to visit the Tawang Monastery, the imposing white fort-like structure standing on the edge of a hill. The courtyard was dotted with the maroon robes of monks. The gentle sounds of the prayer wheel echoed in the air. There was an imposing three-storied assembly hall on one side. Sibsa remembered her last visit there with her mother, when she had seen the huge golden statue of Lord Buddha, reaching up to the first floor.

Once, she flew over a group of dancers wearing elaborate costumes with masks and performing the yak dance. Sibsa joined them by dancing on the carpet herself!

Yet the one place she really longed to visit was Mumbai — to see her father.

It had been more than a year since she had last seen him. She missed him. He would play with her, carry her on his shoulders, make her laugh. How was she supposed to imagine all these things?

She also found it hard to picture the sea, the tall buildings, the dazzling lights and the crowds that her father spoke about, as she had never been out of Arunachal.

Sibsa and her mother would make a weekly trip to town to call her father, as they didn't have a telephone at home. He would tell Sibsa that he was saving money to come and visit them soon. He didn't tell her that after sending money for her school and other expenses, there was not much left to save.

One day, Sibsa returned from school to find a bare table top. She searched frantically for her flying carpet. When she couldn't find it, she ran to her mother in the kitchen.

"Ma, Ma! Have you seen my flying carpet? Has it flown away?"

"Calm down, Sibsa! Khunsum Aunty from next door has taken it for the arts and crafts exhibition at Itanagar. She has a stall there and had promised to display a few of my handicrafts. I was not going to give your carpet, but she insisted, saying it was very different. Anyway, it will only be on display, and we will have it back in two weeks."

Sibsa was very upset. "How could you do this? It was my carpet! You had given it to me. I will never talk with you again!" she started shouting and stormed out of the house.

"Nan wa ga de – le? Where are you going?" called out Sangey.

Sibsa did not go far. She sat under a tree behind the workshop. Anger had given way to tears. When her mother found her, however, she had stopped crying. "Will I really get it back?" she asked, her voice a bit shaky from all the crying.

Sangey nodded.

Sibsa saw her mother's anxious face and kissed her on both cheeks. "I am sorry for yelling at you, Ma."

Sangey smiled, took her daughter in her arms and carried her home.

A few days later, Sibsa was playing outside when three strangers arrived at the workshop — two men dressed in suits, and a lady wearing a sari.

Sangey invited them inside. They introduced themselves as officials from the Government Crafts Centre. They presented her a letter and went on to explain its contents in a mix of English, Hindi and Monpa.

Sibsa heard their animated voices and went to see what it was about.

"Your carpet in particular is very unique and best represents the region," the lady was saying. "We would like to send you to Mumbai for the All India Handicrafts Exhibition. It is a rare opportunity to showcase your talent."

"Thank you so much, Madam. But Mumbai is so far away, and my daughter is very small. I cannot leave her alone."

"Oh, you can take her along too. We will take care of all expenses, including air tickets."

The moment they left, Sibsa came running to her mother. Sangey lifted her up and spun around.

"Your flying carpet is taking us to Mumbai, Sibsa. We will meet your father soon!"

So, finally, Sibsa's carpet did fly . . . even if rolled up in an aeroplane!

THE LOOM PEOPLE

Most women weave, and every household in the village has its own weaving set that is quite basic — a simple reed loom and a semi-curved bamboo tube.

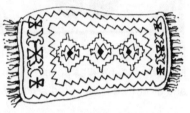

The Monpa and Apatani tribes, as well as the Tibetans settled in the area are skilled carpet weavers. Black, yellow, dark blue, emerald and red are the preferred colours, combined in wonderful ways to create dragon, geometric and floral designs on high quality carpets. Some of the geometric patterns are drawn from Tibetan Buddhism. For a long time, the colours for dyeing the wool came from vegetables, plants, tree barks and seeds. But these days, synthetic dyes and chemicals are commonly used. Carpets that were once woven exclusively for the home are now so popular that they are sold commercially.

The people of Arunachal Pradesh also weave attractive fabrics. Each tribe and sub-tribe has its own range of patterns. Besides cotton and wool, they use fibres from the bark of trees, goat's hair and human hair for weaving! The locals, especially the tribals — the Tangsa, Adi, Apatani, Nyishi and Monpa — still prefer to wear their ethnic clothes. This keeps handloom weaving alive and encourages it to adapt itself to contemporary tastes. If you happen to be wandering the markets, look out for Sherdukpen shawls, Apatani jackets and scarves, Adi skirts, jackets and bags, Mishmi shawls, blouses and jackets, and Wancho bags.

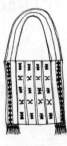

Maharashtra

STAGE TO SCREEN

The French Lumiére brothers introduced motion pictures to India with six soundless short films at Bombay's Watson's Hotel in 1896. The hotel still stands as the Esplanade Mansion in the Kala Ghoda area of Mumbai.

Mumbai is still the land of 'filmi' dreams. But well before the arrival of Hindi films, Marathi theatre was popular. It has lost audiences to TV and cinema, but the actors and directors it nurtured are now some of the brightest sparks in the film industry.

◀◀ REWIND

The region, once called Dandakaranya, goes back to the 3rd century BCE, when Nags, Munds, Bhils, Mahadeo Kolis, Gonds and Warlis lived here. Over the years, Aryans, Shakas and Huns came from the north by land. Others came by sea, thanks to the long coastline. The mix of races may have led to the distinct physical features of a group of people who have fair skin and light brown or greenish eyes.

The Jews arrived around 2000 years ago. Sassoon Docks in Mumbai was built by an influential family of Baghdadi Jews from Iraq.

Most of Maharashtra's history is the story of the Marathas, at the peak of power under Shivaji.

After Independence, there was a demand to unify all Marathi-speaking regions under one state. But Dr B.R. Ambedkar, lawyer and political leader, didn't believe that language should determine statehood.

KOLHAPURI COUTURE

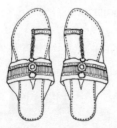

The sturdy, handstitched leather chappals we call Kolhapuri, are actually made in Athani! Embellished with raw silk, crystals, embroidery and beads, they are being hot-footed by the fashionable in Italy, Australia, Japan and Sweden. Giving swish and style to a simple slipper is not only great business sense but empowers the women engaged in this craft.

SILKEN SPLENDOUR

When Greek traders came to Paithan in around 200 BCE, they took back gorgeous Paithani silk saris in exchange for gold and precious stones. One sari can take from a few months to a few years to weave, and cost Rs 6000-Rs 5,00,000!

COASTAL CUISINE

Konkani and Varadi cusine, though quite different, use a lot of seafood and coconut and peanuts and cashewnuts. So too kokum, a deep purple berry with a pleasing sweet and sour taste. Chilled kokum kadhi and kokum sherbet are perfect for a hot summer's day, and good for the stomach!

IT'S A DUCK?

No, Bombay duck is no duck, no bird at all! It's a lizardfish! Locally called bummalo or bombil, it is usually dried and salted before it is ready to be cooked. And always transported in airtight containers. Why? Because it smells very, very fishy!

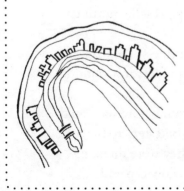

LUNCH COMING!

If you don't get your dabba lunch on a particular day, you're plain unlucky. Because the Mumbai dabbawalas make less than one mistake in six million deliveries! About 5000 dabbawalas pick up some 2,00,000 lunch boxes and drop them off at offices and homes using various modes of transport — and are always on time!

CAVE CULTURE

The Ajanta caves near Aurangabad go back about 2000 years, when 30 caves were carved into a colossal horseshoe shaped rock in the Sahyadri hills, with little more than hammer and chisel. That's probably why it took 600 years to create all of them. Buddhist monks lived, taught, painted and sculpted in these caves, some of which have exquisite mural paintings.

RECLAIMING RAIGAD

Kille Raigad, the 'king's fort'. This royal abode of Chattrapati Shivaji Maharaj, the glorious capital of the vast Maratha Empire, has seen the changing chapters of history down centuries.

Coming to its geography, the hill fort is perched on a sheer vertical wedge sliced off from the surrounding Sahyadris and separated from these same mountains by a deep valley. Though in ruins, it seems as unconquerable today as it must have been over 300 years ago.

But now the great fort had been beseiged — by a band of monkeys!

The monsoons had ended and the monkey season had started. The simians were creating havoc among the tourists. Not happy with snatching packets of chips from backpacks, they were now grabbing the backpacks as well. They took sunglasses, mobile phones, cameras . . . anything and everything.

In the valley below the fort was a village called Pachad, the base from where the steps to the fort began.

Troubled by both the antics of the monkeys and the loss of tourists, the villagers had tried several times to catch the monkeys or shoo them away. But the monkeys were too smart and too swift for them. The local administration had been notified and had acted in typical style, putting up a signboard saying 'Beware of Monkeys'.

It seemed like the monkeys had established their rule at the majestic Kille Raigad. They would have continued their reign of terror had it not been for a clever girl and her brave friends.

Pallavi lived in Pachad and had learnt to climb even before she could run. She and her mates would easily climb the 1500-odd steps to the fort, to have a picnic among the ruins. But the last time they were there, a monkey had snatched away little Golya's favourite yellow cap and deterred them from going there again.

"The monkeys have to be stopped!" declared Pallavi.

"This is the tenth time you've said that," said Amit.

"You know the elders have tried and given up," said Rupali. "They are now saying that the monkeys are ghosts, disguised as monkeys to frighten us."

"Don't you think it would be easier for ghosts to frighten everyone as ghosts, than as monkeys?" shot back Pallavi. "These are just excuses!"

"But Pallu tai, they took my nice topi," grumbled little Golya.

"Hoy. Yes. So they have to be stopped!" said Pallavi, glaring at Amit who muttered "Eleven" under his breath.

Their next meeting was more fruitful. Pallavi had a plan which she discussed with her friends. Convincing Rupali was a bit difficult, but at last she decided to join them.

They set out early in the morning for the fort. On reaching the top, Pallavi took them to first pay their respects to Shivaji at his samadhi, and then to the Jagdishwar Temple to pray to Lord Shiva for success. She put an orange tilak mark on each one's forehead — for blessings and luck, she said.

"Is all this really necessary, Pallu?" said Amit, who was a year older than Pallavi but usually accepted her leadership without question.

"Hoy! This is war! We are going to reclaim Kille Raigad from the enemy, the monkeys!" declared Pallavi, pumping her fist in the air.

"Are we going to play war-war, Pallu tai? But I didn't bring my sword!" said Golya, jumping about excitedly.

"I don't know if it was a good idea to bring Golya. We can still send him back," said Rupali.

"They took my topi! I am staying," said Golya, stamping his foot.

The children set about their plan. They chose the road leading through the former marketplace to lay the trap. The two sides of the road had rows of what looked like neat geometrical patterns – in reality, the ruins of shops. It was the ideal place to hide and watch out for the monkeys.

They borrowed a big empty drum from one of the canteens nearby, and placed it in the middle of the road. Covering the top with hay, they placed a few fruits on it.

The waiting was the hardest part, but finally three monkeys arrived. They circled the drum once or twice, eyeing the fruits, then jumped on top of the drum. The hay gave way and the monkeys fell inside!

"Quick, we have to close the lid!" said Amit, rushing out. But before he or the others could get near, the movement of the monkeys in the drum made it fall, and it was now rolling down the marketplace . . . towards them!

The children hurriedly got out of the way. The drum hit a wall and stopped. The monkeys jumped out and escaped out of sight.

As they walked down the steps, Pallavi felt like a defeated general who had let down her army. Golya seemed to be the only one who had enjoyed the adventure — or misadventure.

"When are we going to catch them again, Pallu tai?" he asked Pallavi earnestly.

"Never, I hope!" commented Rupali.

"If only we knew where those monkeys go off to," said Amit. "We could at least find some of the things they have taken."

"You know that nobody has been able to find that out. Following them is impossible," Rupali replied.

By the time they reached the last few steps, another idea was already brewing in Pallavi's mind. Her friends agreed to her new plan quite readily, as they did not have much to do this time.

The main role was reserved for the village stray. Getting the dog to follow the monkeys seemed like a brilliant idea to Pallavi. The stray, on its part, was happy to get some attention and food from the children, and it trotted behind them to the fort the following morning.

Pallavi laid open a biscuit packet on a flat rock and the dog had just started munching on it when, suddenly, a monkey pounced on it and snatched it away. Startled at having its snack taken away, the dog began chasing the monkey, barking loudly. The monkey was joined by its friends and they ran, chattering angrily but watchful of the dog.

The children followed at a little distance. But the monkeys outsmarted them again. They climbed up a tree and threw the hard seeds hanging from the tree at the dog. The poor creature yelped and fled. The monkeys jumped down and disappeared once more.

The four friends were sitting on the steps of their village temple later that evening, when Golya announced: "Amit dada, Roopa tai, Pallu tai, I have an idea!"

"What is it Golya?" asked Amit, wearily.

"Let us take a lion to the fort to shoo away the monkeys!"

The other three burst into laughter.

"I don't know why you're laughing like babies," said Golya, offended.

But Golya had raised the spirits of the group. Pallavi's mind began ticking again and she came up with yet another idea to put a stop to the monkey menace.

"Are you sure this plan will work?" asked Rupali, as they climbed the steps once more the next day.

"That is the fiftieth time you have said that," teased Amit.

"If it doesn't, Golya has come prepared to fight them," laughed Pallavi, pointing to the shiny toy sword he had stuck under his belt.

They were in the open ground called Holi Cha Mal. Pallavi carefully spread out a plastic sheet and pinned it to the ground with stones.

"It's time to open the can," she said in a low, ominous voice.

Amit yanked open the tin can he was carrying with him. It was full of a thick orange paste — tilak paste! Something about it had stayed in Pallavi's mind after the earlier visit to the temple. It gave rise to her new plan. The friends had prepared the sticky paste early in the morning, by mixing ghee with orange sindoor powder.

"Try not to get it on your clothes," warned Rupali, as they spread the paste with sticks on the plastic sheet. Then they coated a few bunches of bananas with the same paste, and laid them out on the now saffron coloured sheet.

The group watched, hiding at a distance, as five monkeys arrived for the feast and landed on the sheet, one by one. They pulled out a few bananas and ate them.

Then, as suddenly as they had appeared, they grabbed the remaining bananas and took off.

Pallavi, Amit, Rupali and Golya ran out of their hiding place. The monkeys had left a trail of orange handprints, footprints and tail-marks to follow, just as the children had planned!

The prints led them through the Nagarkhana Darwaja — the great door leading to the Raj Sabha, the royal court, where the monkeys had, thankfully, avoided going near the statue of Shivaji. Instead they had jumped off the wall on the right and entered one of the minarets.

The children had to retrace their steps and take the longer route to reach the base of the minarets.

Pallavi saw the footprints leading from the tower to the Ganga Sagar Lake and had a sudden moment of panic — what if the monkeys had entered the lake and the paste had been washed off? But the monkeys were in no mood for a bath. The saffron prints bordered the lake, and could be seen going down the rocky slope.

"Oh, no! We can't follow the monkeys now, the slopes are too slippery," cried Rupali.

"Tar kaay zala! So what! There are steps nearby," said Pallavi. "Come on, let's not give up now!"

Golya ran ahead, followed by Amit and Pallavi, while Rupali trudged behind. They had crossed the Hatti Talao or Elephant's Lake when Golya gave a shout: "Banana skins, banana skins!"

"What colour are they?" asked Amit, rushing down the steps.

"Orange!" yelled Golya.

The monkeys had obviously taken a snack break here. Their orange prints now continued down the steps.

The children reached the imposing Maha Darwaja, the main entrance that curved blindly in a design to confuse enemies. The children at this point were confused themselves, as the prints had become lighter and ended in roundabouts as if the monkeys had gone around in circles. Was this to mislead any followers? Were they really so smart?

"Let's spread out and look around. They couldn't have just disappeared into thin air!" said Pallavi.

Amit went back up the stairs, Rupali continued down and Pallavi and Golya looked inside the main gate again to see if they could find any clues.

"I think I've found something!" said Rupali, running up and out of breath. She led them a little way down the steps and pointed to a cave in the rocks. There was a tiny orange smear at the entrance.

The children were puzzled. They had passed the cave many times before — it seemed small and had hardly any depth. If the monkeys were in there, they would have been easily visible from outside.

Pallavi now examined it closely and found a small opening at the back of the cave. It was hidden by moss and ferns, easy to miss.

"That's it! The monkeys must have gone through there!" she said excitedly. The friends crawled through the hole one by one and landed in a kind of short passage that turned and led into a larger cave. A bright light shone on them and made them squint. Huddled around it were the monkeys.

"Ramu kaka's new LED torch!" muttered Amit. "He showed it to me just the day before it was stolen."

They looked around the cave. The roof was just high enough for them to stand up straight. The rocks jutted out in many places, but some sharp edges seemed chiselled off, as if this place had been in regular use at some time.

"How many more secrets does Raigad have?" thought Pallavi. "Could this have been a secret meeting place or a hiding place for treasures?" Her eyes fell on something glittering in a heap in one corner and she moved towards it, signalling to the others to follow quietly. The monkeys seemed unconcerned by their presence, happy to play with the torch, rolling it around on the floor.

As Pallavi moved closer to the heap, she realised it was a collection of things the monkeys had stolen — bottles, caps, bags, scarves, umbrellas, watches, chains, trinkets…

All of a sudden, Amit, who was near the mouth of the cave, alerted them to the sound of footsteps. Had someone followed them there? The children quickly hid in the shadows and waited, holding their breath. A short, stout man entered the room, and the light from the torch momentarily fell on his dirty, unshaven face.

"Oi! Kai — what is this? What are you sitting here for, you good for nothings!" he shouted gruffly.

The children were horrified. Was he talking to them? Pallavi had to clamp her hand over Golya's mouth to stop him from answering. Rupali covered her own mouth to stop herself from screaming.

"Always lazing around!" the man continued. "Go out and bring me more stuff. Chala, go — chhoo! The monkeys obediently ran out of the cave.

The man picked up the torch and moved towards the heap. He opened a box that was hidden somewhere behind it.

"Wah! Gold chains, mobiles, cameras! Time to sell this lot!" he said and suddenly laughed out loud. "What did they call me . . . a useless monkey trainer? Ha ha! Aata paha, now see, how my monkeys are making me rich!"

"So the trainer is the real culprit behind all the thefts. He must not get away!" thought Pallavi. But what could they do?

She shifted slightly, and realised she was standing on something rough. Was it . . . ? A light bulb flashed in her head! The man seemed quite busy transferring all the loot into a bag, so she quickly whispered her idea to her friends.

The man heard a movement and turned around, just as Pallavi stuck a sword in his stomach and shouted, "Hands up!" In the flickering light of the dimming torch, Golya's toy sword seemed real enough. Also, taken by surprise, the thief had no time to think. He did as he was told.

Quickly, Amit and Rupali tied his hands and feet with the rope Pallavi had been standing on. Golya held the torch close for them to see clearly.

Most of the villagers turned up to see the police drag the thief away. The monkeys, too, were caught when they returned to the cave and later released in the jungle by forest officials, where they would, hopefully, go back to behaving like regular monkeys.

The four friends began picnicking once again at the fort.

"Pallu tai, we won the war, didn't we?" asked Golya.

"Hoy! And we recovered your crown," grinned Pallavi, putting Golya's yellow cap on his head.

Raigad had been reclaimed!

ON GUARD

In the sea, on hills and on plains, they once stood guarding kingdoms. The 350 or so forts of Maharashtra are a reminder of the martial Marathas and Shivaji their leader, who was a great builder of forts. He was a great conqueror of forts as well. The story goes that he trained a monitor lizard, called Yeshwanti, to first scamper up the walls of unclimbable forts with a rope and secure it so the soldiers could climb up easily!

Other rulers built forts too. And what a variety they make together. Raigad, Shivneri and Panhala are built up high so as to spot approaching enemies. Forts on plains, as in Ahmednagar, have deep moats around with drawbridges that would be pulled up in times of attack. Coastal forts like at Bassein, controlled by the Portuguese, gave a sweeping view of the sea and land. And island forts, such as Sindhudurg, were built to guard the coast.

The Murud-Janjira is another island fort that sits amidst sparkling water, just off the coastal village of Murud in Raigad district. Unlike most of Maharashtra's forts, it had no great military beginnings, but was just a small wooden structure built by a Koli fisherman chieftain in the 15th century CE. After that it was occupied mainly by the Siddis, also known as Habshis, who came from Abyssinia or Al-Habsh, modern Ethiopia. The history of this fort marks how the western coast of India saw a fusion with cultures from across the Arabian Sea. The name of the fort is in fact a mix of the Konkani and Arabic words for island — 'morod' and 'jazeera'.

Delhi

WHICH DELHI?

Delhi is said to have been the seat of power 11 times before now. Starting with the Pandavas' INDRAPRASTHA in about 2800 BCE, there was DHILI and LAL KOT of the Tomars, Prithviraj Chauhan's QUILA RAI PITHORA, Aibak's MEHRAULI and Khilji's SIRI. Tughluq rulers built TUGHLUQABAD, JAHANPANAH, and FEROZABAD. Humayun built DINPANAH, Sher Shah Suri had SHERGARH, and the Lodhi Gardens has the remnants of the Lodhi's centre. Shah Jahan's SHAHJAHANABAD is today's Old Delhi. And finally, the British asked Edwin Lutyens to build NEW DELHI.

◀◀ REWIND

BCE Delhi has been inhabited continuously since the 6th century BCE. There are architectural relics here of the Mauryan emperor Ashoka from about 300 BCE.

1192 The Afghan warrior Muhammad Ghori defeated the Rajput ruler Prithviraj Chauhan.

1206 Ghori's slave Qutubuddin Aibak established the rule of what is called the Delhi Sultanate. It had several rulers and dynasties from Central Asia and Afghanistan.

1526 The Mongol-Persian Mughals took over, with Babur as the first emperor and some very famous ones after him, like Akbar.

1857 The British captured Delhi from the Mughals, and shifted their centre here from Calcutta.

1947 At midnight on 15 August 1947, Jawaharlal Nehru unfurled the Indian flag at Red Fort and New Delhi became modern India's capital.

KING OF ALL  Alphonso, Mallika, Amrapali, Himsagar, Malda, Chorasya, Dhaman, Dhoon, Gelchia... More kings, who rule tastebuds! Meet them all at Talkatora, at the International Mango Festival held each summer.

FLOWER SHOWER

When the rains arrive after summer, flower sellers celebrate Phoolwalon ki Sair or Sair-e-gul Faroshan. Reflecting the happy mix of cultures that Delhi is, a procession starts from the Hindu temple of Goddess Yogmaya through Mehrauli Bazaar to place sheets of flowers on the dargah of Muslim saint Khwaja Bakhtiyar Kaki.

FOREST IN THE CITY

Perhaps the only forest within an Indian city is the Delhi Ridge. In the 14th century, Emperor Feroze Tughluq fenced off an area and planted hundreds of trees because he wanted a hunting ground. Watch out for leopards! And monkeys, palm squirrels, foxes, jackals, wolves, blackbucks, chinkaras, nilgais... And about 200 species of birds — flycatchers, woodpeckers, barbets, vultures, crested serpent eagles, booted eagles, great horned owls... Don't forget the binoculars!

MIX AND MATCH

Conquerors from Persia brought with them the art of miniature painting, blue pottery, and exquisite zardozi embroidery in gold and silver that is still done in the little lanes of Old Delhi. And local influence on the Persian language gave birth to Urdu.

— Seeing is believing —

I collect things,
Art and planes, coins and rings.
What am I?

Ans: A museum, of course! Delhi has more than 20 — for trains, dolls, stamps, aircraft and modern art. The Delhi Metro Museum at Patel Chowk is the first such museum in the world in an operating metro station.

THE DISCOVER DELHI HUNT

Want to go on a treasure hunt?

A DISCOVER DELHI HUNT?

Put on your shoes! Pick up your clues!

It's my Birthday party,

and it's all over the city!

– REHAN KHAN

Saturday, 23 Feb, 9 a.m.
Starting point:
A-1204 Central Park,
Golf Course Road, Gurgaon

The race was Saba's idea. She had dropped by at her cousin Rehan's house in the middle of a heated discussion about how to celebrate his eleventh birthday.

Rehan's family lived in an upscale apartment in Gurgaon, the posh Delhi suburb. There were at least half a dozen malls nearby, and his parents thought it would be nice and convenient to have a birthday party at a newly opened one. Rehan thought malls were boring.

So the arguments went on and Saba was well into it. At 14, she too was tired of malls and mall-hopping, so she understood Rehan. Doing something different that was not extravagant was an interesting challenge. She happily assumed charge.

It took Saba just two hours to think of the idea, and two weeks to plan the birthday party.

The nine invitees, mostly Rehan's classmates, arrived at his house on Saturday morning, bang on time, curious about the hunt and eager to start.

Saba explained how it would work: "The hunt will lead you to many places across Delhi, where you may or may not have been to. Hopefully you haven't! I won't be telling you where to go. You have to figure that out from clues given to you. My job will be to take you there. When you get there, there'll be some tasks for you to do, which you'll know then. So…Are you all ready for the Discover Delhi Hunt?"

Ten voices yelled "YEEEEESSS!"

"Right guys, let's go to Delhi! Chalo Dilli!"

Saba gave the children their first clue — an envelope with a card inside that said:

Get the Discover Delhi Hunt off to a flying start, guys!
Now what will you choose, Wapiti or Sukhoi?

There was a symbol on the back of the card — three concentric circles, green in the centre, followed by white and saffron.

"I know! This symbol is called the roundel and is used by the Indian Air Force on its aircrafts," said Vikram, Rehan's best friend. "Should we go to the Air Force base at Palam?"

"Wait a minute!" said Khushi, who was the quizzer in the group. "The second line says Wapiti. That's a very old aircraft. It's more likely to be in a museum."

"That's it! The Indian Air Force Museum at Palam!" said Rehan. He had only recently heard about it.

"Good start!" said Saba. "Let's go."

Kareem Bhai, the driver, was waiting with the Khan family's SUV and they all crammed into it. On the way to Palam, Saba distributed an on-the-move breakfast of sandwiches and juice.

They reached the Indian Air Force museum by 10 a.m. Waiting for them was retired Air Commodore Narendra Sharma, Saba's neighbour, whom she had requested to come. The children had an exciting time listening to the stories Sharma Uncle told them about the Air Force and the planes on display. There were more than 30 aircraft in the hangar – right from those used in World War II, including the Wapiti and Spitfire, to modern ones like the Sukhoi and MiG. Then outdoors there were the Bomber, Canberra and Liberator. Simply awesome!

Saba clapped her hands to call for their attention. "Okay guys, sorry, cadets! Since we are at an aircraft museum, your task is that you will have to fly planes–"

She was interrupted by cries of "Really!", "How can we?", "You must be kidding!" and the like.

"I can explain if you let me finish," said Saba. "I meant paper planes."

"Hey, come on, those are for kids!" scoffed Vansh.

"That's what you think," retorted Sharma Uncle. "Do you know there are world paper plane championships? The participants are adults and call themselves pilots! The Guinness World Record for the farthest flight of a paper plane is 69.14 meters! What do you say to that?"

Saba had downloaded award-winning yet easy to make paper plane designs from the internet. She distributed A4-size papers with instruction sheets and the children were soon absorbed in making them.

These were nothing like the paper darts they threw in school! Once they were ready, Sharma Uncle led them to an empty hangar. One by one, each of them launched their planes and the others marked the distance travelled. They were amazed at how far the planes could fly — though, of course, they were nowhere near the world record!

Sarosh won with a 30 metre throw and was presented with a mock Air Force badge.

Rehan and his friends bid Sharma Uncle goodbye. "Thanks, Uncle! Couldn't have done this without your help," said Saba.

"I enjoyed myself!" replied Air Cdr Sharma. "All the best, cadets, for your next mission," he said, handing an envelope to the children.

The note in it said: *Head to this basti and the Sufi saint will bless you on your birthday!*

"Sufi saint? Must be Hazrat Nizamuddin Auliya. His dargah is in Nizamuddin Basti," said Imran. He had been there once, but the closest the others had got was to Humayun's Tomb nearby.

It took them an hour to drive through the Delhi traffic to get there. It was as if they'd come to another world — far from the skyscrapers of Gurgaon and the wide roads and quiet bungalows of New Delhi, to the rickety houses and tangled lanes of Nizamuddin Basti.

At the heart of this urban village was the sacred tomb of the famous Sufi saint who had lived centuries ago, a pilgrimage centre for his

devotees from around the world. Rehan offered prayers at the dargah with his friends. He liked being there on his birthday, he liked feeling that the saint was blessing him, he liked the peace and calm.

On their way out, Vikram asked, "Whose tomb was it we passed first, near the veranda?"

"Amir Khusro's. He was a poet and scholar, I think. Maybe also a Sufi," replied Imran.

"Another verrry famous Urdu poet is also buried in this basti," added Saba. "You all must have heard of him at least. Mirza Ghalib."

"Oh yes! I've heard my parents talk about him," said Zarine.

"Let's go there, it's close by," Saba said. Giving some instructions to Kareem Bhai, she led them along a boundary wall with lattice screens to a beautiful sandstone courtyard. There were white marble stars on the red floor, and at one end, on a marble square, stood a simple tomb. Across the wall was the Chausath Khamba, a beautiful monument with 64 marble pillars.

"But what is our task here?" asked a restless Arin. "To write poems?"

"You can if you want!" laughed Saba. "Well, actually, a different kind of task. In the olden days, people would celebrate birthdays not just by getting gifts but by giving. So that's what we're going to do here," she went on, more seriously.

Kareem Bhai arrived with two boxes filled with gifts wrapped in colourful paper. With him was a lady and a small group of children — the teacher and nursery students of the municipal school in the basti. The two sets of children stared at each other, curious and a little embarrassed. Then Rehan and his friends distributed the gifts, and squeals of laughter and happy chattering filled the place.

"Thanks Saba. This was a good idea! It feels great, actually," said Rehan.

The others nodded. It was an unusual experience for all of them.

"Right, now get going. If you can't crack the clue, no lunch for you!" sang Saba, handing them the next envelope.

The note in it said:

Are you hungry?

Want to eat something that has a street named after it?

This was easy. Almost all of them knew the answer immediately — Gali Paranthe Wali in Chandni Chowk, a lane known for its mouth-watering paranthas.

"Is Mom okay with us eating street food?" whispered Rehan to Saba.

"She knows," grinned Saba.

In Old Delhi, they parked their vehicle at a distance, and climbed onto cycle rickshas to go through the narrow galis of Chandni Chowk, bustling with people and shops.

"But where are the parantha shops?" asked Manmeet, a foodie, who was the most thrilled about coming here.

"Let your nose be your guide," teased Saba. Sniffing the air, the children reached a row of small eateries.

One of the shop owners greeted them and said to Saba, "We were afraid you weren't coming. It is already 1.30. Par sab kuchh ready hai, ji — everything is ready."

The tables and chairs inside the small eatery had been rearranged in an L shape. There were rolling pins, dough and flour kept on the tables.

"If you want lunch, you have to make it! This is where you learn to make your own parantha from Maharaj-ji, the cook himself," announced Saba. "The one who makes the roundest parantha gets a prize."

The children were hungry and had been looking forward to a scrumptious parantha lunch, but they gamely got to work. First they had to choose a filling. There were 25 varieties — from the common potato, cabbage and paneer to the more exotic papad, almonds and even banana.

Maharaj-ji demonstrated how to roll out the dough into a small circle. This part the group followed easily, though their shapes were not 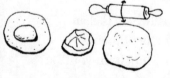 exactly round. He then put the filling in the middle, and sealed the circle into a ball. Dusting some flour on the table, he patted it down and rolled it out into a perfect round shape.

It looked simple enough, but when the children tried, Saba included, things went haywire. The filling kept coming out of the dough as they rolled, or the dough got stuck to the base.

Finally, eleven paranthas were ready in eleven different shapes, waiting to be fried in a big pan of ghee. The only parantha that was anywhere near round was made by a quiet boy called Bijoy, so he won a big box of jalebis, which of course he shared with the others.

The sizzling paranthas were served with tamarind and mint chutneys, potato curry and pickle. The children were amazed they had created something so tasty! Maharaj-ji made more as they ate, and they stuffed themselves till they felt they would burst.

Back at the car, Saba got out a big cardboard box and placed it in front of Rehan. "Your birthday gift!" she said.

The box contained wooden pieces in funny shapes. Closer examination revealed it to be the shape of bones — dinosaur bones! It was an intricate 3D jigsaw puzzle of a dinosaur!

The children started assembling it right away, but quickly discovered that the spine that would hold it together was missing. At the bottom of the box was a message:

*Where in the **History** of Delhi will you get **Natural** dinosaur bones?*

The Children's Museum? A toy store? They were divided about where to go. Rehan noticed that two words were in bold: 'History' and 'Natural'. Of course, the National Museum of Natural History!

The giant dinosaur at the entrance to the museum made the children confident they'd come to the right place. As they stood marvelling at the 160-million-year-old fossil on display, they were joined by the museum's educational assistant who gave them the missing spine of their puzzle. In the activity room, the children re-assembled the dinosaur — it was a T-Rex that stood two feet tall.

They went on a tour around the various sections of the museum. There were lifelike stuffed animals, an interactive section about ecology called Nature's Network, and a model of a big hand uprooting a tree that showed what was happening to trees all around. They went back and forth between exhibits, fascinated by all they saw.

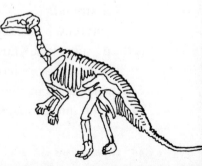

"Jaldi, quick! Your T-Rex is already here, waiting for you!" joked Saba, giving them an envelope when they joined her in the car.

In it was a photograph — of a rather plain canopy with four pillars, standing on a small mound of green.

"This could be anywhere in Delhi," commented Vansh.

"Look closely," said Saba.

When they did, the children noticed the Qutub Minar against the skyline. "Somewhere near Qutub, obviously," said Arin, frowning. They asked Saba to take them there. It was 4 p.m. by now. As they neared the Qutub complex, they were again confused as to which structure the picture showed.

"Okay, one more clue," said Saba, and showed them another picture, of a gate shaded by trees, like an entrance to a park. The group drove slowly around the Qutub area and one of them spotted it. It was the gate to the Mehrauli Archaeological Park which had monuments and ruins over some 800 years, from the eleventh to the nineteenth century.

"Since this place is a photographer's paradise, the clues will also be photos. You have to find the location of this photo. When you go there, you will get the next clue," instructed Saba, giving them a picture and maps of the park.

The photo showed the remains of a wall, with a perfectly intact arch. The children consulted the map and walked towards No. 1 Balban's Tomb, where they could see some arches in the distance. They passed the courtyard and found the octagonal tomb in ruins — but all the arches in good shape!

"Hey, what's this?" cried Bijoy. His sharp eyes had spotted something hidden in a crack and only partly visible. An envelope, their next clue!

The picture in it was of a red and blue floral pattern, the kind found in old carpets. It looked delicate and beautiful in contrast to the jagged relics all around.

"This must be somewhere indoors. It looks like a carpet or floor pattern," suggested Khushi.

They could see a red sandstone dome further ahead. The map said it was the Jamali-Kamali mosque and it seemed to be in better condition. The group spread out looking for the pattern. Beside it was the tomb of

Jamali and Kamali. Their graves lay next to each other, and the walls were decorated with exquisite blue and white tile work.

"Upar dekho! Look up!" said Zarine, pointing to the ceiling. It was covered with the same intricate red and blue design they were looking for!

"Great! What is our next photo about?" said Manmeet hunting for an envelope.

"The last clue is the first picture you saw in the car," replied Saba, running up to them.

"Where've you been?" asked Rehan, guiltily. So busy was he with the hunt that he hadn't actually noticed she hadn't been with them for a while.

"Oh, I just sat down for a bit," Saba replied. "Come on, who's got the first photo?"

Vikram fished it out of his pocket. It was the one of the canopy. The children remembered seeing it on the way to the mosque.

"Let's race!" said Sarosh, and all of them ran up the hillock to the canopy called Metcalfe's Folly.

There, under the dome, stood a small table with a cake!

"Mom, Dad, Nanu, Nanijaan!" exclaimed Rehan, seeing his parents and grandparents come up from the other side.

Everyone sang "Happy birthday" as Rehan cut the cake.

"Well done, Saba beti! Proud of you!" said Rehan's parents.

And ten voices yelled, "THANK YOU, SABA! YOU ROCK!!"

CAPITAL PLUS

Delhi now refers to the National Capital Territory of Delhi (NCT). It includes New Delhi, Old Delhi, the Cantonment and other areas. The NCT plus surrounding towns from other states, such as Gurgaon, NOIDA, Faridabad, Ghaziabad, Baghpat and more, make the National Capital Region (NCR). The idea of the NCR first came up in 1962. The purpose was to build a major business area around Delhi while reducing pressure on the main city.

Andaman & Nicobar Islands

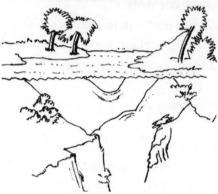

FIRE DOWN UNDER

These 572 islands are actually the highest peaks of a mountain range under the Andaman Sea! It makes them vulnerable to earthquakes and volcanic eruptions.

The small 3 km wide Barren Island is the only active volcano in South Asia. Dormant for 177 years, it woke up and erupted in 1991. Since then it has rumbled some more, now and again, even as recently as in January 2017!

The 2004 tsunami was caused by an earthquake that began in Indonesia and carried all the way underwater to these islands and the Indian coast.

THE FIRST PEOPLE

Only about 34 islands are permanently inhabited. The indigenous people are some of the oldest living communities in the world — the Andamanese, Sentinelese, Onge, Jarawa, Shompen and Nicobarese. The Karen, a hunter-gatherer tribe, were brought in by the British as labour from Myanmar.

From what is known, there are two families of Andamanese languages, Great Andamanese and Ongan. There is Sentinelese as well, about which almost nothing is known because the tribe has remained fiercely independent and isolated. Sadly, most of the Great Andamanese languages are nearly extinct.

THE NEW PEOPLE

For a long time, the Andamans could only be reached by sea, mainly from the ports of Kolkata and Chennai. There must have been many people from there who came to the islands, because Bengali and Tamil are the major languages spoken here, followed by Hindi and Telugu. Tourism and work now bring in a mix of people from all over India.

INTRUDERS

What we call 'development' has threatened the Jarawas. It began with the building of the Andaman Trunk Road through their forest in the 1970s. Outside settlers and poachers exposed them to diseases they had never known, and their numbers dwindled to around 300. The tribals were also being shown off as exotic attractions. But now all tourist activities are banned within the Jarawa Reserve.

◀◀ REWIND

10th century	The Chola king, Rajendra Chola used the Andaman & Nicobar Islands as a naval base.
17th century	The Marathas used them as a base and grew as a major maritime power.
1756	The Danish colonised the Nicobar Islands and called it New Denmark.
1778-84	New Denmark was taken over by the Austrians who thought Denmark had given it up. They renamed it Theresia Islands.
1789	The British set up a naval base on Chatham Island and slowly took over all the islands. Indians who fought in the 1857 War of Independence were sent here as prisoners. Later the British built the notorious Cellular Jail in Port Blair, the current capital, to which they sent all political prisoners of the freedom movement.
1943-44	Port Blair was the headquarters of Netaji Bose's Azad Hind government.

FLUTTER BY

225 species of some of the most spectacular butterflies of the world live on these islands. Mount Harriet National Park is where to find them, and a variety of moths as well.

The Homecoming

"We are going to have a great adventure! I just know it!" declared Kanmani, as she boarded the ferry to cross over to Baratang.

Her older brother Kumaran, and their friends Udita and Mohit, agreed excitedly.

A thrilling three hour bus ride through tribal reserves and dense tropical rainforests had heightened their expectations. Now, as they approached the island surrounded by lush mangroves, tall evergreen trees and mysterious canals, they could sense that Baratang would hold out its promise of adventure.

Although Kanmani's family was from Tamil Nadu, she was born in the Andamans and had always lived there. She had not, however, seen much of the islands.

"The best beaches are near Port Blair. We don't need to go anywhere else," had been their father's constant refrain. But now even he admitted that Baratang was a different experience altogether. One of the main islands of the Great Andaman group in the Bay of Bengal, Baratang was still a largely undiscovered place, full of natural wonders not found in other parts of the Andamans.

On reaching the forest guest house, they started making plans for sightseeing. The caretaker's nephew owned a tourist dinghy, a small boat with an outboard motor, and Kanmani's father arranged for the boy to take them all around in the afternoon.

But, like showers on a sunny day, Kanmani's father had a work-call and he had to leave immediately for Rangat, a town further up north in the Middle Andamans.

"Aiyyo, Appa, do you really have to go?" groaned Kanmani.

"It's really urgent, kanna. And don't forget I am on an official trip," replied Appa. "Anyway I'll be back tonight and we'll go to see the caves tomorrow. Today you all play in the guest house."

"But the entire day will be wasted! Can't we go out on our own?" asked Kumaran.

"Please, Uncle!" implored Udita and Mohit.

"Okay, you can go out for a walk. But don't go too far. Bye, I'm off!" he said and left.

The children found an old carrom board and played indoors till afternoon.

After a heavy lunch, they decided to go for a walk and made their way to the jetty. A few small boats were anchored there. A teenage boy from one of the dinghies approached them: "Are you Selvan babu's family? I am Bikram. My kaka is the caretaker of the guest house. He asked me to wait for you."

"Oh! I am Kumaran, this is my sister Kanmani, and Mohit and Udita are our friends."

"Can I take you somewhere? Selvan babu isn't coming?" Bikram asked.

"He had to go to Rangat on work today. But yes, can you take us for a ride in your boat?" said Kumaran, the idea hitting him only just that moment.

His sister and friends were surprised, but soon caught on. "Please take us, Bikram! We were so looking forward to exploring the place," they pleaded.

"If your father is okay with it, then theek aachhey, fine," said Bikram. He did not notice the shuffling feet and shifty looks of his young customers. "The limestone caves and the mud volcanoes will take 45 minutes one way..."

"No, not the caves. Appa wants to see those too, so we'll go there tomorrow. Can you take us for a ride through the mangrove creeks now?" requested Kanmani.

"Theek aachhey. But only for a short trip. Now get in and wear your life jackets."

Bikram spoke Bengali with Hindi thrown in. He had also picked up a little English from tourists and had no problem with the mix of English and Hindi the children used while speaking to him.

They headed towards a narrow creek. The mangrove shrubs growing on either side had joined to form a canopy of twisted branches and dense

leaves, casting deep shadows through which the afternoon sun barely filtered through.

The water glowed like emerald and jade, and the only sound they could hear was the steady humming of their motor boat.

But it was the mangrove roots, rising above the water, which made the children gape in astonishment. Long, winding and knotted, they formed a tangled mesh that entirely covered the muddy ground they grew upon. "Like tentacles of a monster!" whispered Kanmani to Udita.

"The roots are like that because they grow in salt water and have to face the tides," explained Bikram.

"That's true, they may look like monsters, but they are guardians, protecting the land from storms and preventing soil erosion," added Kumaran.

After about 20 minutes through the creek, Bikram turned around to go back. Just then they heard a soft splash in the water. In front of them was something that looked like a piece of floating log. But then they saw it — a spiky tail swishing through the water towards them.

Slowly, the face of a crocodile surfaced. A second and much larger one emerged a few seconds later, blocking their path completely.

"CROCODILES!!" shrieked Udita.

The saltwater crocodiles were massive, at least five metres long. They had dark, leathery skin covered by sharp scales, and were staring at the children with their dangerous yellow eyes.

"Orrey! We can't go back this way!" exclaimed Bikram, and did a quick U-turn. "Come to the centre of the boat everybody!"

The crocodiles glided behind their boat.

"They are following us! Will they attack us?" panicked Udita, just as one of the crocodiles opened its jaws to reveal a frightening set of pointy teeth.

"I don't want to find out... hold tight," said Bikram, and dashed ahead at full speed. Only after they had reached the end of the mangrove tunnel and joined a wider waterway, did he slow down.

The children scanned the waters for any sign of the crocodiles, but they seemed to have been left behind.

"I've never seen crocodiles from this close before," muttered Bikram, a bit shaken. "Let's get back home now."

He took another route that was parallel to the one that turned out to be crocodile infested, but soon reached a dead end. He made his way back and now entered a bigger channel. They could see islands on the other side shrouded by dark forests. The nearest one was long and tapering, beyond which the channel opened out to the sea. The water was rough and the currents were stronger. Bikram steadied the boat and made a slow circle in the water.

"Why are you going round in circles? Don't you know the route? You must have been through these waters hundreds of times," said Kumaran.

"Not really. It's just been a month since I started taking the boat out alone. Actually, my elder brother was supposed to show you around. He couldn't make it today, so he sent me," replied Bikram sheepishly.

"Why didn't you tell us that before?" said Kanmani.

"Oh God, what if the boat overturns!" screamed Udita.

"Orrey! I know how to ride the dinghy well and have taken people for short trips alone," defended Bikram. "If it hadn't been for those crocodiles, we would have got back long ago."

"Wait a second, are you trying to say you don't know how to get back?" asked Mohit.

Bikram shook his head.

"It means we are lost!" cried Kumaran.

LOST!

The word echoed silently in Kanmani's head. She thought of her mother and her home in Port Blair. When an official trip to Baratang coincided with an unexpected holiday from school, Appa had decided to take his family along. But their little sister was still too small, so their mother stayed back with her and suggested they ask their neighbours Mohit and Udita instead.

"It is our fault too," Kumaran now said. "We came without Appa's permission."

"Why didn't *you* tell me before!" said Bikram sarcastically.

"It's no use blaming each other. Why don't we just keep moving along? We may find our way back," suggested Mohit.

"We can't. There is very little fuel left. We can't waste it. We have to be sure which direction to go. Don't worry. I am sure another boat will come along any moment and guide us back," said Bikram, wondering why they hadn't seen one till now.

"Why haven't we seen one till now? Are there no tourists?" Kanmani echoed his thoughts, making Bikram jump.

Either that or . . . Bikram dreaded to think of the other option — a storm warning! But the sky looked clear as of now. "Yes, there must be no tourists," he said, trying to appear calm.

"When Appa gets back at night he will be so worried," sobbed Kanmani.

The group fell silent. The boat bobbed with the tide which carried them a little further.

Then suddenly Udita jumped up. "Look there, a beach!" she cried, pointing to the tapering island. A sandy patch was now visible at its tip.

Kumaran cheered up, "Hey, can we go to that island? There could be people living there who could help us."

"My brother told me that most of these islands are unoccupied. And some are Jarawa reserves, like the one you crossed to get to Baratang. They don't like intruders," Bikram cautioned.

The children had read about the Jarawas in their school textbooks. They were one of the native tribes of the Andaman Islands, which migrated from Africa thousands of years ago. They shunned contact with the outside world and lived a nomadic life, hunting and gathering food. Only about 300 remained, inhabiting the western coast of South and Middle Andaman, which are protected Jarawa tribal reserves.

"But Bikram, we are stranded in the middle of nowhere. What else can we do?" reasoned Kanmani.

At that moment, three figures appeared on the beach. They were Jarawa boys, with curly peppercorn hair and faces plastered with clay.

"It will get dark soon. This is our only chance," urged Kumaran and Mohit.

Bikram had to agree. "Fine," he said finally. "We can make a short stop to ask them for directions." He navigated the boat towards the beach, but had to halt a few metres away.

"I can't go any closer. There are many rocks here — the boat could get damaged," he said. "And I dare not go around them, the current is very strong and we could be pushed to the open sea."

The Jarawa boys had seen the boat and were staring at them.

"They might be able to hear us from here," said Kumaran and shouted: "Baratang, Baratang."

"It's not loud enough. We all have to shout together," said Mohit. "On the count of three ... 1 – 2 – 3 ..."

"BARATANG! BARATANG!"

At once one Jarawa boy pointed to the left, one pointed to the right and the third stood lost in thought.

The children stared at them. "Is this some kind of a joke?" Kumaran wondered aloud.

"I think they didn't hear us properly. We should try again," said Udita.

The Jarawa boys were also discussing among themselves.

"Look!" shouted Kanmani.

All three boys were pointing to the sky.

"I knew it would be no use asking them," Bikram sighed, and put his head in his hands.

"Maybe they are pointing towards a star for direction," said Kanmani, not ready to give up.

"The sun is just about setting. How will there be stars now?" said Mohit.

Yet Kanmani scanned the skies. "Well, there is nothing ... just a few birds."

Kumaran looked up. "Yes, all I can see is a flock of parrots ..."

"Parrots! Did you say parrots?" exclaimed Bikram, and looked up too. And sure enough, a group of colourful parrots flew closer into view above them.

"Quick! We have to follow them," said Bikram. "Thank you!" he shouted to the Jarawa boys and waved. The boys waved back.

"Why are we following the parrots?" asked the children.

"They will lead us to Parrot Island and that's close to the jetty. I know the route from there," said Bikram, gathering speed.

The parrots were soon out of sight, but other flocks kept appearing. The children followed the path the birds took. Green, yellow, red — parakeets of all hues and sizes were heading in the direction of the mangrove swamps.

The squawking of the parrots was getting louder and louder, but the shrubs arching over their heads blocked their view.

Then suddenly, as the boat veered to the left, what a spectacle there was in front of them!

Hundreds and hundreds of parrots circled above a small, flat mangrove island, a symphony of birds flying together, their shrill voices coming together to create an untamed (if raucous) melody!

"This is Parrot Island! All the parrots return home at sunset everyday. They are calling out to each other to signal that it is safe to land," Bikram told his enchanted companions. He also told them that this patch of mangroves looked different because the parrots ate the tops of the mangrove plants, leaving it to look like a freshly cut hedge.

As the sun set behind the island, many more groups of parakeets flew in for their evening nesting. The birds now looked like a swarm of dancing shadows against the crimson sky. They continued their synchronised performance till the last group arrived, only then did all the parrots touch down.

It was a magical homecoming, a perfect finale to an afternoon spent drifting in unknown waters.

"Chalo! Come on," said Bikram, revving up the engine. "Time for us to go back to *our* homes!"

MIGHTY MANGROVES

"If there are no mangrove forests, then the sea will have no meaning. It is like having a tree with no roots, for the mangroves are the roots of the sea."

— A saying in southern Thailand

Mangroves are trees or shrubs that grow in shallow and muddy water. The saltier the water, the better! That's why they grow on the fringes of creeks, backwaters, shorelines and estuaries. They can be recognised easily by their tangled masses of arching roots visible during low tide.

One-fifth of India's mangrove forests are in the Andaman & Nicobar Islands. They buzz with animal life of all kinds — crab-eating monkeys, monitor lizards, saltwater crocodiles. They are an ideal spawning ground for fishes, shrimps and crabs.

What these forests are particularly good at is preventing the erosion of soil. How? By slowing down the force of water and wind as they pass through. In a sense, they help to reclaim land from the sea. In 2004, these mangroves saved the North Andaman Islands from complete devastation by the tsunami. The thick forest surrounding the islands worked like a protective shield to minimise damage and save many lives.

Gujarat

DINO PRINTS

Want to see a Dino limb in a rock? Or a 65 million-year-old egg fossil? Head out to Balasinor, where dinosaurs once roamed. In nearby Raiyoli, fossils of about 10,000 dinosaur eggs have been found, making it one of three largest dinosaur fossil sites in the world. Palaeontologists believe that at least seven species of dinosaurs lived around Balasinor. One, discovered in 2003, belonged to the Tyrannosaurus Rex family and was called Rajasaurus Narmadensis, the 'princely reptile from the Narmada'!

ROARING NEIGHBOURS

Gir National Park is the only natural habitat for wild lions other than in Africa. The local Maldhari community has lived here for generations, side by side with the kings of the jungle.

SALT WHITE

An endless stretch of packed white salt, spectacular in the moonlight. That's the Rann of Kutch, when dry. When it rains, this world's largest salt desert is submerged and thousands of Greater Flamingoes migrate here to breed. The Gurkhur or Indian Wild Ass found here looks like a cross between a donkey and a horse and sprints at 80 km an hour!

I COME FROM GUJARAT

Mahatma Gandhi was born in a white house near the Arabian Sea in Porbandar. His thoughts are relevant to the world even today, a century after he was born.

Physicist Dr Vikram Sarabhai launched India into space. He set up the first rocket launching station (TERLS) in the country near Thiruvananthapuram.

Ela Bhatt founded the Self-Employed Women's Association of India (SEWA) and set a trend for the financial empowerment of women in India.

Gujarat was one of the main centres of the Indus Valley Civilisation. Lothal was the site of India's first port (around 2400 BCE). The world's oldest reservoir is in Dholavira.

The state gets its name from the Gujjars, who ruled around 700-800 CE.

The Mauryas, Shungas and Sakas reigned here, and the Greeks made an incursion. Among the local dynasties, the area prospered under the Solankis.

With ancient Persian links, the region came under direct Muslim rule for 400 years.

In the 1600s, the Dutch, French, English and Portuguese had bases along the coast and acquired settlements — Daman & Diu and Dadra & Nagar Haveli.

Parts of Gujarat came under British rule but there were dozens of princely states.

MMMM! MILK!

Operation Flood was a cooperative movement that became the largest dairy development programme in the world and put thousands of dairy farmers in charge of their livelihood. It was started in Anand by 'India's Milkman' Dr Verghese Kurien, who went on to create the Amul brand of milk products. The 'utterly butterly' Amul girl is one of the most successful mascots ever for an ad campaign!

GLANCING THROUGH GUJARAT

Palitana in Gujarat is the only place in the world with more than 900 Jain temples, that too at a height of about 2000 ft.

Bhongas are traditional houses in Kutch. Cylindrical in shape, with conical roofs, they are said to be earthquake resistant.

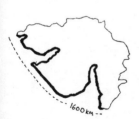

At 1600 km, Gujarat has a longer coastline than any other state in India.

The Zoroastrians came from Persia (therefore called Parsis) in the 8th-10th century CE to escape persecution, and settled here. They adopted the local language and way of life and are a prominent community today.

📖 Bapuji's Little Followers

Gyan Sagar Vidyalaya High School, better known as G.S.V. High
School, was in central Ahmedabad. This was the old part of the city, with
bustling street bazaars, tourist attractions, and the centuries-old pols with
clusters of houses huddled together. Somewhere in the middle of all this
stood the school's long rectangular structure, with three floors of
classrooms opening out onto corridors. A cemented courtyard was the only
open space in the school, where morning assembly was held every day.

Behind the school, separated by a narrow lane and a high wall, was a
maidan of about the same size as the school building. The school had been
using this field as a playground for many years, and it had come to be
known in the area as G.S.V. Grounds.

There was a small side gate through which the students would go to
the maidan. It was here that they were stopped one day by a uniformed
guard. He said they were not allowed to enter as it was "private
property". The children were confused and went to Pathak Sir, their
principal, who said he would look into it.

The next day, at assembly, Pathak Sir announced: "I have some
disturbing news. The playground — *our* playground — has been sold by
the government to a wealthy industrialist, G.R. Mehta. It seems a big mall
will come up there."

There were shocked gasps and groans.

"That ground was promised to us by the education minister himself,
when he was chief guest at our Annual Sports Day, four years ago. I have
been trying to contact him since yesterday, but all I get are officials who
say they are unaware of any such promise. Moreover, they are asking us
not to use the grounds," Pathak Sir continued.

There was now an uproar in the assembly.

"Sir, we cannot allow this. A children's playground is far more
important than another shopping mall," said Mrs Chokshi, the history
teacher. All the students clapped and cheered in agreement.

The principal motioned them to be quiet. "I know it is a grave injustice, but what can we do?" he said, looking troubled.

"Why don't we call the police, Sir," a few students suggested.

"I did call them. They don't want to interfere in this matter. We are up against powerful people. We cannot fight them."

"We can, Sir. Gandhiji said that with satya and ahimsa, we can bring the whole world to our feet," came a voice, earnest and clear.

Everyone craned their necks to see who had spoken.

It was Mohan, a boy from Class 7. He stepped forward and spoke directly to the principal: "Sir, we visited Sabarmati Ashram last month and learnt all about Bapuji's life and his struggle for freedom. He brought down the powerful British Empire through satyagraha and non-violence. Can't we get our playground back?"

The visit had left a deep impression on Mohan. A busload of boisterous boys and girls had made their way to the Gandhi Ashram, on the banks of the Sabarmati river, for a history excursion and picnic. The peace and quiet of the ashram, the green cover — home to chirping birds and scampering squirrels — the whitewashed cottages, the ebony statue of Bapuji deep in prayer, all had a calming effect on the children.

They walked around the ashram, paying their respects at the Upasana Mandir, the prayer ground. They saw Gandhiji's cottage, Hriday Kunj, with the spinning wheel, writing desk and floor cushion in the corner, just as it used to be when he lived there. A sculpture of three monkeys made Mohan laugh, but his teacher explained its meaning — see no evil, hear no evil, speak no evil.

At the museum, lifelike oil paintings and hundreds of photographs told the story of Gandhiji's life — his childhood, his days in England and South Africa and his role in the Indian Independence movement. The children learnt that it was from this ashram that Bapuji had started the famous Dandi March to protest against the British salt tax — an idea so simple, yet so brilliant, that it caught the world's attention.

Mohan had felt truly inspired then, and now was determined to fight this new injustice. With Pathak Sir's permission, the next morning he and a group of children from various classes, accompanied by a few teachers, walked from their school gate to the busy main road and reached the actual entrance of the ground. They stood there holding placards and shouting slogans: 'Give Our Playground Back', 'We Want Justice', 'Right Against Might' . . .

The gates to the grounds were locked, and there was nobody around. Some curious passers by stopped and stared at the protestors, but mostly they were ignored. Finally they returned to school, dejected.

"We won't give up, children, though it won't be easy," Pathak Sir told them. "I had gone to Mr Mehta's office to talk to him, but was told he was in a meeting and couldn't see me. The minister is away in Delhi. His officials scoffed at our protest and said it will have no impact on the government."

"More students will be joining us tomorrow, Sir. We will carry on till we get justice," Mohan spoke up bravely.

The next day, as the children hurried to school, they noticed a flurry of activity at the maidan — a stage had been erected, chairs were arranged in rows and people were entering the grounds. The narrow lane between the school and the grounds was jammed with vehicles.

Pathak Sir was in a state of nervous excitement. "I have found out that today is the bhoomi puja for laying the foundation for the building. The minister and Mr Mehta will both be coming for the ceremony," he said. "This is our chance to meet them and resolve the matter."

Mohan and his classmates went behind the principal, carrying their placards. But they couldn't get far. A battalion of policemen had cordoned off the area near the main entrance to the grounds, and no one was allowed there without a valid pass.

They waited, crammed behind the barricades. Soon they saw a convoy of cars with the minister and the industrialist entering the gates. The students began raising slogans but were drowned out by the noise of traffic, police whistles, and music that began blaring inside the grounds. When they asked the police to let them through, they were rudely told to leave.

"Enough, children. Please go back. Also, if I am alone I may be allowed inside," Pathak Sir said firmly. Reluctantly, the children retreated to school.

Mohan lingered in the second floor corridor. They had given up too soon, he thought. Bapuji would not have. "Forsake not truth even unto death," he had said.

Looking towards the grounds he could see it was now filled with people. The minister had begun his speech. Even if Pathak Sir had managed to get inside, he would definitely not be able to reach anywhere near the platform.

"We have to catch their attention," thought Mohan, "Pun kevi rite? But how?" He was trying to think, when some papers a teacher was correcting flew out of the classroom towards him. He caught them as the teacher hurried out exclaiming, "Uff, so windy!"

January was full of such windy days. No wonder Uttarayan, which
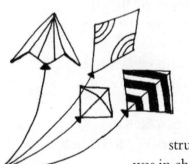
was just a week away, was celebrated with kite flying! Families would be up on their rooftops, flying kites from dawn to dusk. The skies would be filled with kites of all shapes and sizes.

"That's it!" Mohan ran into his classroom bursting to tell his classmates what had just struck him. They then went to Mrs Chokshi, who was in charge during the principal's absence. She gave her approval for the plan and things swung into action under her supervision. The children formed three groups, with five students and a teacher in each. Each group would go to Jamalpur, Kalupur or Dariapur — all famous kite bazaars — and buy as many white kites as they could.

Mohan and some others went to all the other classes and told them about the plan. They divided the students into teams — Message, Transport, Prepare and Launch. The Message and Prepare teams were assigned classrooms, Transport was to wait in the corridors, and Launch was to assemble on the rooftop.

In about 15 minutes, the group that had gone to Dariapur was back. They had got 30 white kites and reels from the market. The kites were taken straight to the Message class, where students were waiting with markers and sketch-pens. But the slogans they had come up with were very long, and would not fit on the kites.

"We need something short, like maybe 'TRUTH' and 'JUSTICE'," Mohan suggested.

"Yes, but we also have to send out a more direct and clear message," said Mrs Chokshi.

"Like what?" asked Mohan.

"Gandhiji's protests had names that always sent out a clear message to the masses — like Non-cooperation Movement, and Quit India."

"Thanks, Ma'am. You've given a great idea!" said Mohan. "Let's write 'QUIT G.S.V. GROUNDS' on some of them," he told the others.

The Transport team ran with the kites to the Prepare classroom, where students tied threads to the kites. This had to be done carefully otherwise the kites would not fly properly. Kites and reels were then taken to the terrace, where Mohan joined the others. All the other teachers were up there too. A student held up high the first kite with 'TRUTH' written on it and gently let go.

The kite began to rise. The girl holding the string slowly released it, then pulled it back. She did this a few times and soon the kite was soaring in the sky.

There were quite a few kites up in the sky when 50 Kalupur kites arrived and were made ready by busy teams for take-off. More Launchers took their positions and released the kites.

Mohan hurried excitedly from classroom to terrace to see how his plan was going. Most of the kites were flying well, but some were getting tangled and cut, even though they were using ordinary cotton reels and not the sharp manja coated with glass powder.

They would need reinforcements fast!

Just then, the final group of students came back. They had gone the farthest, to Jamalpur, the biggest market for kites, but they didn't have anything in their hands.

"What happened? Why aren't you carrying any kites?" Mohan asked, running up to them.

"We couldn't! There were too many! We bought 100 of them," said his friend, just as a tempo entered the school compound loaded with kites. "We got free home delivery!"

Meanwhile, at the grounds, the minister finished his speech and G.R. Mehta took centre stage. A few minutes ago he had noticed, like the others, a few kites flying in the sky. Nobody was surprised, as it was kite flying season. But now, from the front of the stage, he could see that they were all white kites and their numbers had suddenly increased. There were more than 100 kites flying overhead!

Every now and then, a kite would get cut off and fall to the ground. People were looking at kites and murmuring among themselves, the buzz growing louder by the minute. Clearly, the industrialist was losing his audience. At that moment a kite floated near the dais.

Mr Mehta bent and picked it up. It had 'JUSTICE' written on it in bold letters. He asked his security guard to go find a few more kites. The others had the messages 'QUIT G.S.V. GROUNDS' and 'TRUTH' on them.

"Aa shoon chhe? What are these? Where are these kites coming from?" the minister asked.

Meanwhile, Pathak Sir was hurrying back to school with the same thoughts.

The minister's secretary was sent to investigate and soon came back with the answer: "From the school next door!"

Mr Mehta was determined to get to the bottom of the matter himself. He gave the mike to the next speaker and left the stage quietly. The minister unwillingly accompanied him to the school next door. As they approached the school, they could see children on the rooftop, flying kites.

Pathak Sir came up to them. He finally had his chance to remind the minister of his promise to give the maidan to the school. He also told both of them how they had been unreachable the past two days. Indicating Mohan, who had been filling him in on the kite-flying plan, the principal said, "Mohan here has been motivating us to use Gandhian strategy in our fight to keep our playground. Flying kites with messages was inspired by the Dandi March, he says. It certainly is ingenious in its simplicity! He is Bapuji's innovative little follower!"

Mr Mehta looked on in astonishment. Then he said, "Mohan, I am so happy to meet you. Pathakbhai, it is heartening to know that children these days still relate to Gandhiji. I am so sorry, I didn't know you were trying to reach me. And of course, I had no idea about the land being promised to the school."

"How this confusion happened, mane khabar nathi, I have no idea," the minister said apologetically. "I will make sure the maidan is handed over to the school."

This time, the minister did keep his promise.

THE HOUSE THAT GANDHI BUILT

Sabarmati Ashram takes its name from the river Sabarmati on whose banks it stands. It was first called the Satyagraha Ashram as it reflected the movement toward non-violent resistance launched by Gandhiji.

Spread over 36 acres, it was a wasteland full of snakes, but when it was being built the brief was not to kill them. Non-violence was the firm founding block.

Mahatma Gandhi stayed at the ashram from 1917 until 1930. It is now preserved as a memorial to him. Hriday Kunj, the small cottage in which he lived with his wife, Kasturba, displays many of Gandhiji's things — writing desk, walking stick, spinning wheel . . . The Gandhi Smarak Sangrahalay, a beautifully designed museum within the ashram, has about 34,000 letters written by or to him, over 6000 photographs, and 210 films.

The ashram was a place to bring together those committed to non-violence as a means to get India freedom. From here Gandhiji launched the famous Dandi March on 12 March 1930. Along with 78 companions, he set briskly off on the long walk to Dandi in protest of the British Salt Law, which taxed Indian salt to promote the sale of British salt in India.

Before he set off on this march, it is believed Gandhiji said he wouldn't come back to the ashram until India was free. With this march, the journey to freedom did indeed begin in earnest. It sparked off more mass movements. Tens of thousands of freedom fighters filled British jails.

India finally became free on 15 August 1947 but Gandhiji was assassinated just a few months later, on 30 January 1948. He never did return to Sabarmati Ashram.

Jharkhand

I COME FROM JHARKHAND

Birsa Munda was a tribal hero who fought against the oppression of his people by non-tribal locals as well as the British. He led the Munda Rebellion in the late 19th century and was a fearless freedom fighter — all this before dying in jail at the age of 24.

Deepika Kumari of Ranchi was once World No. 1 in archery. In the 2010 Commonwealth Games she won two gold medals — one each in the individual event and team recurve event.

Mahendra Singh Dhoni was 'Captain Cool' of the Indian cricket team that won the 2011 World Cup and the 2007 ICC T20 World Cup.

LAND OF FORESTS

Jharkhand was first the southern part of Bihar. The Jharkhand Mukti Morcha, a political party, started a movement for a separate state. In 2000, Jharkhand was created, the name meaning 'land of forests'. And yes, the region is covered with dense forests, as well as hills, waterfalls, springs and lakes. Over 32 tribal groups live in Jharkhand, mainly Santhal, Oraon, Munda, Ho, Kharia and Bhumij — almost a third of the state's population.

STEEL CITIES

Jamshedpur had India's first private iron and steel company and was also the first planned industrial city. Founded by the late Jamshedji Nusserwanji Tata, it is also known as Steel City or Tatanagar.

Bokaro Steel City is where the largest steel plants in India can be found, and several other medium and small industries.

UNDERGROUND

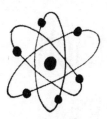

Jharkhand has nearly half the country's minerals — iron, coal, mica, copper and bauxite among the most important. This is why the area had one of the country's earliest industrial belts in the Jamshedpur-Dhanbad-Bokaro region. Indiscriminate mining, however, is threatening forests.

RESERVED

The vast Singhbhum Elephant Reserve is the first elephant reserve in the country. It was created in 2001 under Project Elephant to conserve the habitat and increase the population of the Asiatic Elephant — which, of course, is the state animal.

IN COLOUR

Delicate and beautiful, Kohvar and Sohrai paintings are done by women, during weddings and harvest time. Only natural colours are used — neutral earth shades, red oxide from stone, red ochre, kaolin white and manganese black — to create motifs and symbols that are similar to the ancient cave art found in the area.

⎯ Tree of Life ⎯

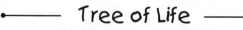

I cover entire forests, grow straight and tall,
My leaves make plates and bowls, big and small,
Buddha and tribals, I am important to all.

Do you know what tree this is? The tribals believe that their protector, Goddess Sarna, lives in it. During February-March, in basant or spring, when the tree gets new leaves and flowers, they celebrate Sarhul. The flowers stand for friendship and bonding, and the priest gives some to every home. Then comes the fun part. They sing and dance and drink handia or diang, the intoxicating rice wine that has been offered to the goddess!

Ans: This is the sal tree (*Shorea robusta*). It oozes a honey-gold gum on its trunk that works as glue when softened with water. The tree also has medicinal properties — maybe that is why it's worshipped? Buddha is said to have been born under a sal tree.

THE MARK OF A CHAMPION

Susmita Sahu had a dream — to be the world champion in archery. But this was a dream she saw with her eyes wide open.

She was an outstanding archer. After using the traditional bow and arrow for a few years she was now training in recurve, the only form of archery featured in both the Olympic and Asian Games. And for the first time Susmita was representing Jharkhand in the ongoing National Inter School Archery Championship at the Birsa Munda Athletics Stadium at Ranchi.

She had breezed through the qualifying rounds and was seen as the favourite to win the championship. The finals were scheduled to have been held the next day, but unexpected heavy rains led to them being postponed by four days. Susmita knew that winning the gold would pave the way for her future in her beloved sport.

It was in this happy frame of mind that she went to school the following day. She had been excused from classes till the competition was over, but this sudden postponement gave her a chance to meet her friends. She had not met them for ages, for she had been too busy training.

As she entered her classroom her smile disappeared. In place of the teacher stood three boys — three troublemakers of her class. One of them, Ballu, was saying, "This will teach you not to go complaining to the teacher about us."

"No! Don't do it! Please!" said a pleading voice that Susmita instantly recognised.

She stormed into the room just as Ballu was about to pour a bottle of ink on her best friend Rimi's notebook. Rimi was crying.

In a swift move Susmita snatched the book from Ballu's hand, startling him and making him spill most of the ink on his shirt.

The class, which had been watching in silent horror, now laughed at Ballu and began to boo him.

"That will teach *you* not to bully others," said Susmita.

Ballu's two friends were already retreating. The three boys were afraid of Susmita, afraid that she would make them the target of her arrows as she had once jokingly warned them.

Ballu too turned to go, but then suddenly whirled around and pushed the teacher's big table onto Susmita.

CRASH!

Susmita was on the ground with the heavy table on top of her.

As her friends helped her up, Susmita was seething with anger. She wanted to run after Ballu and hit him hard. "Humse dar ke bhaag rahe ho ka? Running scared from me, are you?" she shouted behind him.

Rimi held her back. "Are you hurt?" she asked anxiously.

"Hurt? No. I'm fine," Susmita said, even as she felt something was wrong with her right arm. She tried to move it, and cried out with the searing pain that flashed through.

Things happened swiftly after that. The teacher and the principal were called. They informed her parents and she was rushed to hospital, examined by doctors and given first aid. All through, Susmita tried in vain to convince first her friends, then her principal, and then her parents that she was fine. She had not even looked at her arm again in the belief that if she paid no attention to it the pain would go away. Now, as she waited for the doctor to arrive with her X-ray report, she said a silent prayer.

"It is not a fracture," said the doctor, coming straight to the point.

A wave of relief broke the silence in the room as everyone started talking at once.

"Thank you, doctor!" said Susmita. She tried to do a polite namaste to him and found she couldn't bend her right hand. The medicines and ice-pack had numbed the pain, but she saw that her upper arm was badly swollen.

"Hai, Ma! My arm! How will I . . ." she cried out to her mother, then turned to the doctor. "Will I be able to do archery, Doctor?"

"Of course!" said the doctor reassuringly. "It is a muscle injury, you see. You will not be able to bend that elbow for a while because of the swelling. But don't worry, your arm will be completely all right in a week or two!"

"But the finals are in three days! THREE DAYS!" Susmita cried, making a desperate attempt to bend her elbow. At once the pain began to surge back. How would she fit an arrow to the bow, let alone hit a target with an arm like that? For the second time that day Susmita felt the world crash down on her.

Later in the evening her friend Rimi came to see her at home. Susmita had just woken up from a nap. The swelling was still bad. Rimi tried to cheer her up with the news that Ballu and his friends had been suspended from school. Susmita was glad Rimi didn't go on about how she could always "win the competition next year", like everyone else. That was too far off. She had to play now, in a few days. "Winners don't quit and quitters don't win!" she said to herself fiercely.

The day of the championship finals arrived. The atmosphere at the mega stadium at Ranchi was electric, with supporters from the participating schools rooting for their teams. Among the names of the participants for the under-15 girls' category that boomed from the loudspeakers was: "Susmita Sahu, A.C.E. Public School, Jharkhand!"

Susmita walked to the field with her bow and quiver of arrows, and took her position at the shooting line. Thirty metres away was the target face. It had 10 concentric rings, two rings each of white, black, blue, red and yellow, scored from 1 to 10, from the outermost circle to the centre. She scanned the crowded stadium and smiled when she spotted her schoolmates in their maroon uniforms cheering for her.

There were seven more girls standing at the line. To her right was her closest competitor — a girl called Sweety from Maharashtra, who was stiff competition for Susmita, and who stared incredulously at Susmita's right hand covered with an arm guard.

The signal was given for the competition to start. The winners would be decided on the basis of knockout eliminations, where after each round the two lowest scorers would be out of the competition. Normally 15 arrows had to be shot in all, but because of the time constraint (it still threatened to rain) the number had been reduced to nine — three arrows in three rounds or 'ends', as referred to in archery. The time limit for each end was two minutes.

Sweety scored 7-7-8. It was now Susmita's turn. She took her stance and raised the bow . . . with her injured hand! Keeping the bow level with the target, she fitted the arrow onto the string with her left hand and drew the string back fully to the side of her face. She looked down the arrow focusing entirely on the centre of the target — and then let go. The arrow flew to the face and she scored 9 points! The next two arrows came quickly one after the other, scoring 8 each. Susmita was the highest scorer in this end!

The crowd was stunned. Everyone knew that Susmita was a right-handed archer. She had clearly injured that hand, and her rivals and their supporters had been hoping it would pull her out of the competition. Instead, she had managed to score so well with her left hand!

But this was no miracle. Susmita had been determined not to allow an injury to come in the way of her dream. "Don't practise until you get it right. Practise until you can't get it wrong," she had heard somewhere. So she had practised continuously with her left hand for the past three days till she couldn't go wrong.

Thankfully her recurve bow was light yet powerful, needing lesser force. On the first evening she had struggled to even position the arrow on the string. By the second day the arrows were flying all over her garden. By the evening of the third day, the left hand had been trained enough to hit the target every single time.

On the field, six girls remained. Sweety, with three straight 8s, was the highest scorer in the second end. Susmita's scores were not good this time. With 7-7-5 she just managed to scrape through to the final end.

There were now just four left in the competition, and based on their scores they would be awarded the gold, silver and bronze medals. Susmita's two minutes started. She steadied her bow arm and took aim. The first arrow hit the red ring and got her 7 points. She had to do better if she wanted gold.

"If I can believe it, the mind can achieve it!" Susmita repeated to herself as she took aim again. She tried to block out the increasing pain in her right arm and focused on the target. "I can do it!" she thought, as she released the arrow. It hit bullseye! She had won 10 points!

She positioned her final arrow. "Su–smi–ta! Su–smi–ta!" the crowd chanted. One more good shot and she would win! She drew back the string... but it hadn't even gone all the way back when her injured arm jerked involuntarily under the strain and the arrow flew off. Susmita saw her gold dreams blurring as the arrow hit black on the target.

"Susmita Sahu from A.C.E. Public School, Jharkhand!" This time the name was announced for the victory ceremony.

Susmita stepped forward to accept her bronze medal. The stadium reverberated with applause. Susmita waved to the crowd. The disappointment on her face was not just for missing the gold, it was also for missing the opportunity that came with it.

The medals were being presented by none other than the former archery world champion, Mukesh Hansda, who was the chief guest for the event. He congratulated Susmita and said, "Miss Susmita Sahu, it is my privilege to offer you a scholarship to train in my archery academy."

Hansda Academy had coached many international and Olympic level athletes. Training there was every aspiring archer's dream, but the fees were high and admission was strictly for gold medallists.

It was only when she found the world champion waiting questioningly for a response from her that Susmita actually realised what he'd just said.

"S–sir, th–that is the reason I wanted to win the championship so badly! B–but isn't the opportunity only for the winner?" she finally managed to say.

"Yes, it is true we admit only gold medallists — or shall I say, champions," smiled Mukesh Hansda. "And the mark of a champion is not whether you fall, it is whether you get back up again. If in your condition you can get bronze, I am sure when you are in form nothing can stop you from being the greatest champion in the world!"

ON TARGET

"Champions aren't made in gyms. Champions are made from something they have deep inside them — a desire, a dream, a vision. They have to have the skill, and the will. But the will must be stronger than the skill."
— Muhammad Ali, the legendary boxer

Archery is a target sport that requires immense concentration and strong technique. In modern competitive archery, the target face has ten concentric rings with different points for hitting each — the highest, of course, for bang centre. The archer stands in a particular stance (such as open or closed), points the bow downwards, fits the back of the arrow into the bowstring (called nocking), raises the bow, aims and releases the arrow.

Arrows these days can fly at more than 240 km an hour. Arrows in mythology could do a lot more, like drying up a sea, or turning into serpents!

Archery was known to many ancient cultures the world over. The tribal people of Jharkhand are natural archers. Many of the promising young archers from these communities are selected to the leading Regional Training Centre, the Tata Archery Academy in Jamshedpur. Deepika Kumari was one such girl. She grew up in a little village in the midst of sal, mahua, teak, lac and mango trees. She would aim at mangoes as a child and not be satisfied till all of them were on the ground! Deepika picked up a professional bow and arrow for the first time when she was 13. Two years later, in 2010, she was the Commonwealth gold medallist in recurve archery!

Telangana

⏪ REWIND

Excavations suggest that the region dates back to the Palaeolithic Age. The Kakatiyas (950 CE-1323 CE) and the Qutb Shahis (1496-1687) were important dynasties that ruled here. Then came the Nizams in the 18th century, who were great patrons of art and culture. After Independence, Andhra Pradesh was the first state to be formed on the basis of language and in 2014, Telangana was carved out of it as a separate state.

SCROLL ART

Cheriyal scroll paintings are peculiar to Telangana, and combine Kakatiya and Mughal Nakashi traditions using vibrant organic colours. Once used for mythological retellings, this art form can be seen on temple walls, and now even on wooden toys.

FLORAL FESTIVAL

Flowers for the mother goddess... During the nine-day Bathukamma festival, women arrange flowers in a conical stack to make it look like a temple gopuram.

TELUGU

is one of the oldest Indian languages and the third most spoken language in the country.

is one of the four classical languages of India along with Sanskrit, Tamil and Kannada.

is also spoken in Andhra Pradesh, and pockets of Karnataka, Chattisgarh, Maharashtra, Odisha, Tamil Nadu, Puducherry.

D A K H A N I

is the widely spoken form of Urdu, a curious mix of Turkish, Arabic, Persian, Telugu, Kannada, Konkani and Marathi. This singsong dialect derives from the original Dakhani spoken in the courts of Deccani Muslim rulers around the 14th century.

I COME FROM TELANGANA

Filmmaker Shyam Benegal paved the way for 'middle cinema' in India with 'Ankur' in 1974. His award-winning movies show up the stark realities of contemporary India, its patriarchy, political hypocrisy, and the helplessness of the common man, often with a touch of humour.

Tennis star Sania Mirza and badminton ace Saina Nehwal are both from Hyderabad.

A 'SOUND' FORT

Golconda, about 11 km from Hyderabad, was actually golla konda, 'shepherd's hill'. The fort here built by the Qutb Shahis has a unique sound system. If you clap your hands at the entrance, it can be heard a kilometre away — a useful warning signal! The buildings of this period are a combination of Persian, Pathan and Hindu styles, called Deccani architecture.

The Golconda area also had one of the country's richest diamond mines. The Koh-i-Noor, the Darya-e-Noor and the Hope diamond were produced here.

WHOOOSH!

Head to the Nagarjuna Sagar dam to watch the Krishna river gush down the world's tallest masonary dam – 124 m high and 1.6 km long.

Fire!

I may be thin, wrinkled and small,
but if you put me in your mouth,
the fire brigade you will have to call!

Ans: Chilli. Telangana food is spicy hot, and Warangal is a major chilli producing district in the country.

THE COOLEST DONKEY

Tina was about to go to bed when she heard her friends calling out to her.

"Raja has had an accident, come soon," they cried. Tina rushed with Suhana, Viju and Rahul to where Raja lived. He was lying down with a bandage on one of his legs. When he saw his friends, Raja greeted them with his usual "Dainchu dainchu!"

The little donkey lived in the bylanes of Hyderabad. He worked very hard for his master, Abdulla, pulling a cart with heavy loads all over the city. The neighbourhood children loved Raja and often came to play with him in his rundown shed of bamboo sticks and tin roof, right outside Abdulla's house. Tina, Suhana, Viju and Rahul were his special friends. They would get him carrots and hay on which he liked to chew.

"What happened to Raja, Abdulla Chacha?" Tina asked Abdulla.

"A fool on a bike came very close to my cart and my poor Raja stumbled and fell. He has hurt his leg and back," said Abdulla. Seeing their worried faces he continued, "Fikar nako. Don't worry. I have taken Raja to the doctor and he will be all right soon."

Over the next few days, Raja recovered. Abdulla realised, however, that though Raja could walk now he would not be able to pull heavy loads. So he decided to sell him. The four friends were devastated.

"Please, Chacha, don't sell Raja. We all love him," they pleaded. But Abdulla did not relent. "If he doesn't help me earn, what use is he to me? Where will I get the money to feed him? I am going away to my village for the next few days, and when I am back I *will* sell him."

Tina was watching TV that evening, still feeling sad, when she suddenly had an idea. She called the others and told them her plan. "I was seeing a movie about a horse and other animals. I thought if Raja could also act in films, then Abdulla Chacha will have money and can take care of him."

"What an idea! But how can this happen? We don't know anything about *how* movies are made or *who* makes them," said Viju.

"But we know *where* movies are made — in Ramoji Film City. We can take Raja there to meet the filmmakers and see if they'll take him in their movies," replied Tina.

"Tina, Raja is just an ordinary donkey, not some film star. Why will they be interested in him?" argued Suhana.

"Yes, if only our Raja could look like a film star . . . like Vajrakanth," said Rahul, looking up from the magazine he was browsing. He pointed to a picture of Vajrakanth, the famous Telugu film star, wearing a silver jacket with shiny sequins on the collar and pockets, a red scarf, and a red hat with a silver band.

"Maybe we can dress up Raja to look like a star. I have an old red hat, we can make Raja wear that," joked Viju.

"My sister has a red scarf," said Rahul, laughing.

"Hey! That's not a bad idea. I have a silver dupatta. My Ammi stitches some of my clothes, I can ask her to make a kind of jacket for Raja," said Suhana excitedly.

Tina hugged Suhana and said "Thanks guys!" to Viju and Rahul, who were looking dazed at being taken seriously.

Over the next few days, Tina helped Suhana and her mother stitch the jacket. They sewed sequins on, and it looked just like the jacket in the picture. The boys decorated the red hat with a silver band and made slits in it for Raja's ears.

Some days later, on a Saturday morning, the children got down to the task of transforming Raja into a film star.

First they bathed him and brushed his tail. They then put the shiny silver jacket over his back, fastening it with laces below and buttoning the sleeves down the front legs. They tied the red scarf around his neck, and finally placed the red hat on his head.

Raja looked grand in his costume!

They set off for Ramoji Film City in the van they had borrowed from Viju's father who owned a grocery store. He had also given them a few carrots for Raja. The excitement built up as they approached the entrance to Ramoji Film City, the world's largest film studio complex. But when they

went to buy tickets to go in, they were told, "No animals allowed." Not knowing what to do, the children hung around. The queue for tickets got longer as more people arrived and it soon got quite crowded.

Suddenly there was a commotion near the road — loud cheering and waving by the people there. A black BMW was slowly making its way through the crowds towards the gate. Rahul pushed his way ahead and caught a glimpse of the person in the car. It was Vajrakanth!

The car came to a halt as a few fans blocked the way trying to take pictures of the film star. The security guards began shouting at them to stand back. Meanwhile, agitated with all the noise, Raja began to bray loudly: "DAINCHU! DAINCHU!"

Everybody turned to see what was causing the racket. Vajrakanth's window rolled down and he motioned with his hand for the four children to come forward.

"What is this? Why is that donkey wearing a costume like mine, I say?" Vajrakanth asked, raising his eyebrows.

"Sir, this is our friend, Raja. He wants to act in movies and be famous like you. He should look like a film star, no? So we dressed him like you, sir," said Tina.

Vajrakanth burst out laughing.

"Daya chesi, please, sir, give him a chance," said Viju.

Vajrakanth signalled to one of the guards, "Let these children come in. The donkey too." Turning towards the children, he said, "Come to the Outdoor Building set."

Proudly, the children and Raja crossed the gates and found their way to Vajrakanth's set. It was the first time they were at a film shooting, and were quite taken aback by the frenzied activity. Some were shouting orders, some were following them, there were people working on the background, the lighting, the camera, the costumes. They spotted Vajrakanth, sitting in his chair and oblivious to his surroundings.

"Cheppandi, tell me, what are you kids doing here? What exactly do you want?" asked Vajrakanth when they came up to him.

Tina told him all about Raja and his injury, and how they wanted to help him.

Vajrakanth offered them money, but the children refused saying that they wanted Raja to be useful and earn his keep.

"I would really like to help," said Vajrakanth, "but right now none of my films need any animal, let alone a donkey." Looking at their dejected faces, he added, "Something could come up though. I'll ask my secretary to contact you ..."

The children cheered up. Vajrakanth asked the spot boy to get them something to eat. They watched the star shoot an action scene, while they tucked into masala dosa and ice cream. Vajrakanth jumped from a high building (with safety cords attached to him) and landed on top of a moving car driven by the villain.

It was all quite thrilling! They thanked Vajrakanth and decided to take a tour of Ramoji Film City before leaving. They saw magnificent gardens, modelled to resemble their famous originals. The hero and heroine of a film could be dancing in the Mughal Gardens of Delhi, and when the coloured lights and fountains came on it would look like the Brindavan Gardens of Mysore. If the movie needed a foreign location, they could prance around in a Japanese Zen garden a little further down!

The children spent some time playing in Fundustan, a dream-like entertainment park for kids. Here everything was larger than life, especially the blue ship and the hop-n-jump snakes and ladders game on the floor. Raja enjoyed all the attention he got from the other children, though he stopped, surprised, in front of the giant blue head of a genie, the mascot!

They saw sets of palace interiors, small towns and streets straight out of another country. There was a school that turned into a police station at the drop of a board, and an airport terminal that looked like a hospital from the back and a church from the side.

In one of the sets, lots of people were moving about and there were cameras and lights everywhere. The setting was of an outdoor restaurant with tables and chairs all around.

"Let's watch another shooting," said Suhana. So they waited.

And who should enter but Vajrakanth!

Looking at their surprised faces, he explained, "The shooting for that film is over for the day. I am here to shoot for an advertisement." A man wearing a white hat came up to him just then to discuss something. Vajrakanth introduced him to the children as the director.

"Sir, could you take Raja also in your ad?" Rahul asked him, seizing the opportunity.

The director looked at Raja. "Enti? What? A donkey! This is an ad for a soft drink. We need someone who is really cool, like Vajra. What will I do with a donkey! Vajra, you now have to take a sip of the cola and say these lines . . . Aiyyo! What is happening . . . STOP THAT DONKEY!"

None of them had noticed when Raja slipped away. He was now chewing on the straw of the cola bottle kept on the table. It looked like he was drinking from it.

"Super! Your donkey is so cool, I say," laughed Vajrakanth.

"Well, well," said the director, suddenly inspired. "Maybe we can use him after all!"

So it was that Raja became a TV star. A super hit! Abdulla was happy with the money Raja made and dropped all ideas of selling him. He even built a nice shed for Raja.

Tina, Suhana, Rahul and Viju sat in front of the TV to watch the advertisement for what must have been the hundredth time…

Vajrakanth and Raja enter a restaurant, both dressed in silver jackets, red hats and red scarves. There is a bottle of cola on the counter. Vajrakanth lassoes the bottle and pulls it towards him. He then flips opens the cap, takes a sip, keeps the bottle on the table and says: "Be cool like me, drink Kool-o-Cola, with a cool refreshing taste and . . ."

There is a slurping sound. Vajrakanth turns to see that Raja is finishing his cola, sipping through a long straw.

The camera zooms in on Raja and a voiceover says, "Why be cool when you can be the cool*est* — drink your Kool-o-Cola fast, or I will finish the rest! Be the coolest, Kool-o-Cola is the best!"

FILM FACTS

Close to 150 films are produced every year in the Telugu film industry which recently completed 80 years since the first talkie film, *Bhakta Prahlad.*

Most of the early films were based on religion and mythology. The first was the silent film *Bhisma Pratighna*, in 1921. Even when sound made its entry in 1931, the themes didn't change.

With their individual styles and body of work, Akkineni Nageswara Rao (ANR) and N.T. Rama Rao (NTR) were the two great stars of their time. They set the trend for the cult following that film actors in Telugu cinema have today.

RECORD SMASHERS

Ramoji Fim City, Hyderabad, is the largest film studio complex in the world.

D. Rama Naidu has produced the most number of films — 150.

K. Brahmanandam has acted in the most number of films in a single language — over 1000.

S.P. Balasubramaniam has the most number of songs sung by any male playback singer in the world — around 40,000 — and the majority of his songs are in Telugu.

Vijaya Nirmala is the female director with the most number of films — 47 of them.

Goa

The beaches of Goa are one of the nesting places for the famous Olive Ridley turtles.

You can also spot long-beaked dolphins in the shallow waters off the less busy beaches.

In the small state of Goa are packed different habitats — shrubs, wetlands, dense forests. In fact, known for its beaches, it comes as a surprise that Goa has a very high forest cover, over a third of its land mass. Most of these forests are in the Western Ghats of eastern Goa. They have been compared to the Amazon and Congo basins for the rich variety of plant and animal life.

SEASHELLS ON THE SEASHORE

The sea creeps even into Goan craft! Shells of different shapes, colours and designs are made into chandeliers, lampshades, curtains, candle stands and trays.

◀◀ REWIND

Goa was part of the Maurya, Satavahana, Chalukya and Vijayanagara empires.

The seafaring Portuguese landed in the early 16th century CE, and thought Goa's natural harbours and broad rivers made it an ideal base from which to control the Eastern spice route. From a small area around Old Goa, their control spread by mid century. Jesuit missionaries led by St Francis Xavier arrived in 1542.

Old Goa or Velha Goa was built by the Bijapur sultans in the 15th century. It was capital of Portuguese India until it was abandoned in the 18th century due to plague.

The Marathas almost defeated the Portuguese in the late 18th century, and the British briefly occupied Goa. But Portuguese occupation ended only in 1961, when the Indian army marched into Goa.

I COME FROM GOA

Mario Miranda was India's first internationally acclaimed cartoonist. His pen and ink cartoons were brilliant and funny, whether about politics or everyday events. He also liked to paint and do murals.

Popular musician Remo Fernandes sings rock, pop and fusion in English, Hindi, French, Portuguese and Konkani. His numbers stand out for the way they combine many different musical influences such as Goan, Portuguese, African, Latin and West Indian.

TILE TALES

Azulejos are hand-painted glazed tiles, an art introduced by the Portuguese who learnt it from the Arabs or Moors who invaded Spain and Portugal. Azulejos comes from the Arabic word meaning 'smooth'. They usually have floral patterns or religious scenes, in yellow, blue and white. They can be seen in monuments, churches and homes, like the Menezes Braganza Hall, the Old Goa church and Chinchinim village in South Goa. This art form died after the Portuguese left, and is now being revived.

Two-wheel ride

It is black and yellow and for a ride you can hire
But it is driven by a pilot and has two tyres!

If you're hailing a cab in Goa, you may find a black and yellow motorcycle pull up. Go for it, it's Goa! You'll have the wind in your hair, the sky above and a 'pilot' for a driver (yes, that's what he's called).

Taxi Driver

PILLION-
PASSENGER

📖 THE MONSTER

Panaji, 8 Feb 2013, midnight

"We've done it! We've created a monster!" yelled Freddy to his two comrades. "Tomorrow we will unleash the beast on the streets of Goa!"

Baga Beach, a month ago

It was a busy evening at Martin's Shack.

This restaurant, right on Baga Beach, specialised in seafood and was a popular place for tourists to hang out. Freddy was serving the orders with a cheerful smile. He did not actually work there. The owner, Martin Pereira, was a distant uncle, his only surviving relative whom he lived with, and Freddy helped out at the shack after school.

Besides, he really liked being there at Baga Beach. The cool breeze and the palm trees swaying in the breeze, the ebb and flow of waves and the speed boats riding on them, the warm sand and the sand castles, the bright sunshine and the lovely sunsets, he liked them all.

Freddy also liked chit-chatting with his customers, who came from all corners of the world. On this particular day, as he gave a gentleman his bill he asked pleasantly, "Hope you are having a good time, sir?"

"Not bad, thanks! But you know what, I would have had a really good time if your beaches weren't so dirty! Everywhere I am lookin' I see plastic bottles and more plastic bottles. You guys will destroy the environment, you know! Don't you care at all?"

Freddy was taken aback. He had been told not to argue with customers, but he was very upset. "How dare he call our beaches dirty!" he thought. The shack was definitely not dirty. Uncle Martin ensured that. The only thing Freddy could not deny was the plastic nuisance. Customers asked for bottled drinking water, and would then leave the empty bottles lying about, scattered outside near the rows of sun beds and deck chairs. It did look unsightly. And though he had heard

about plastic spoiling the environment, he hadn't really thought too much about it. Was it really so harmful?

The next day, he asked his teacher about it.

"Good you brought this up," said his teacher. "And I'm surprised you, and maybe others in this class too, don't know about it. So let me tell you — plastic is very, VERY harmful for the environment. Thousands of animals are killed because they eat or get entangled in plastic waste. Plastic causes flooding by clogging drainage systems. Did you know plastic takes hundreds of years to break down? So plastic bottles that are not disposed of properly cause littering, and they release dangerous gases that cause air-pollution. The thing to do is to reduce the use of plastic and to recycle it. Remember the three magic Rs, all of you — Reduce, Reuse, Recycle."

Freddy was quite disturbed. He knew thin plastic bags had been banned in Goa – that was why Uncle Martin always told him to carry a cloth bag when he went shopping. But what of the hundreds of plastic water bottles that were used and thrown every day? His eyes now began to pick out every bottle lying around, and there were so many!

He began to collect all the discarded plastic bottles in and around the shack. This became a daily habit before closing time. He collected them in big bags, and at the end of the week handed them over to a recycling depot his teacher had told him about.

One day, his friends Savio and Fillip dropped by.

"What man, the Carnival is coming up. What about our plan?" asked Savio.

Freddy had been so engrossed with his new mission, that he'd completely forgotten about their grand plan. The Carnival days had all of Goa celebrating with music and dance and feasting, and the highlight was the parade in each area. Last year, Savio's brother had built a big dolphin float for the parade at Mapusa, and Freddy, Fillip and Savio had danced along with it, waving pom-poms. This year, the boys had planned to make their own float.

They now eagerly pooled the money they had been saving for a year, but were disappointed to find it was just enough to hire the vehicle that would carry the float.

"What about the material to build the float? Where will we get the money for that?" asked Freddy.

"I can't ask Dad," said Fillip.

"I know there are money problems at home, so I can't get any either," Savio said. "This shack's doing well, man. Couldn't you ask Martin Uncle for some money?" he asked Freddy.

"I don't like to ask. He does so much for me already," said Freddy.

"But dude, how are we going to build the float? We'll have to call it off then!" said Fillip.

"Okay, I'll speak to him tomorrow," said Freddy, still doubtful.

The next morning, Freddy called his friends for an urgent meeting. "Guys, guess what, Uncle and I came up with a super idea to use what we have. And he says we'll take part in the Carnival at Panaji, where they have the biggest parade!" he told them excitedly.

Panaji, 9 Feb 2013

People dressed in their best clothes were making their way through the streets that were decked up for the parade. A live band was playing.

King Momo, the Carnival king, led the parade waving to the crowds. His float was an underwater kingdom, complete with mermaids and sea horses! Alongside were dancers in colourful costumes. The crowd cheered them on.

Next came a Goan village market, straight out of one of Mario Miranda's cartoons.

The third float was shaped like a fishing boat with fishermen doing a Konkani dance. This was followed by a model of a huge ant! Then came a beautiful garden with big, colourful flowers and a butterfly that fluttered its wings.

All the floats had their own music with speaker systems, and singers and themed dancers. There was a Goan wedding float with people dancing with masks, as in a masquerade. There was a giant gorilla playing drums, and a 'Save the Tiger' float with a big tiger that actually roared.

The next few floats too may have been good but no one seemed to notice, for their attention was caught by what came behind them. It was the tallest float they had ever seen — almost 30 ft high!

"VHODLO monster! BIG monster!" screamed some children. "PALEY! LOOK OUT!"

A monster it was, but it looked almost transparent! Only when it came closer could people make out that it was made entirely of throwaway plastic bottles.

The body of the monster was itself shaped like one huge water bottle. The head was a dragon's, covered with blue bottle caps. It had wide open jaws, and teeth made of smaller-sized bottles. Horns on the head, big red eyes and a spiked tail that rose into the air gave the monster the look of a devil. It reached out menacingly with its two huge arms (six bottles thick and ten feet long) towards a big globe in front, ready to devour the world.

On both sides of the truck were written 'PLASTIC MONSTER', and in front was a placard that said 'No. 14 – Baga Boys'.

The Baga Boys — Freddy, Savio, Fillip, and a few of their friends — were on another float just behind, which had a big garbage can in the middle. They were asking bystanders to give them their empty plastic water bottles for recycling. Many in the crowd were glad to get rid of their bottles. Playing on the float was a song the boys had composed, called 'Recycle-Recycle', about the harmful effects of plastic on the environment.

The Baga Boys won the first prize for the best float that year! Even better, there were recycling drives all over Goa after this. And the Plastic Monster? It stood guard near Martin's Shack on Baga Beach to make sure no one littered the place with plastic again.

LIGHTS, COLOUR, MUSIC!

February is Carnival time. Introduced by the Portuguese, it was originally meant for Christians and known as Entrudo or 'entry', into the 40-day period of Lent leading up to Easter Sunday. The word 'carnival' comes from the Latin for 'to take away meat' because meat eating during Lent is traditionally a complete no-no.

Himachal Pradesh

CRICKET IN THE SKIES

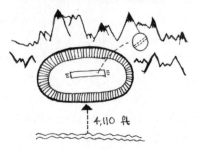

4,110 ft

At the HPCA cricket stadium at Dharamshala, chances are you'll drop a catch — because the spectacular view of the Dhauladhar range of the Himalayas is way more eye-catching! At 4110 ft above sea level, this is the world's highest international cricket stadium, and possibly the prettiest. Chail has the world's highest cricket pitch, built in 1893, at 7200 ft.

I COME FROM HIMACHAL

Nobel Peace Prize winner Tenzin Gyatso, the 14th Dalai Lama, came here from Lhasa with thousands of Tibetans to escape Chinese rule. He set up the Government of Tibet in Exile in the village of MacLeodgunj in Dharamshala district.

Vijay Kumar, who won the silver medal in 25m shooting in the 2012 Summer Olympics, is from Harsore in Hamirpur District.

Actor Kangana Ranaut, winner of three national awards, is from a small town in HP.

SPEAKING UP

Hindi is the official language of Himachal but Pahari is what you mostly hear on the street. With so many communities — Brahmin, Rajput, Gujjar, Gaddi, Ghirth, Kannet, Rathi, Koli and tribal — there are almost as many languages.

COLOUR ON CLOTH

The Himachali cap with its colourful borders and beautiful patterns is worn with pride by the locals. Severe winters made wool weaving a household activity, and Kullu is especially known for its brightly patterned shawls. Even more famous is the Chamba rumal, a square piece of silk or muslin with fine embroidery that looks like needle-painting.

The first tribes believed to have moved up to the hills of Himachal are the Kols or Mundas. Then came the Bhotas and Kiratas.

During the Vedic period, there were several small republics here called Janapadas. These became part of the Gupta Empire, after which several local chieftains, including some Rajputs, went independent.

The Delhi Sultans and the Mughals got control of some of these kingdoms. The Gurkhas of Nepal too came here. Later, many of the local rulers preferred to be friends with the British and progress under them.

28 small princely states first integrated to make the Chief Commissioner's Province of Himachal Pradesh in 1948. The new state of Himachal Pradesh, with more areas added was formed only in 1971.

TAKE YOUR PICK!

Himachal is the fruit bowl of India. Oranges grow in the valleys, grapes in the hills, and mangoes, litchis, guavas, strawberries, apricots, peaches, plums, cherries and pears where it is a little warmer. Wild flowers dot the hillsides, while gladioli, carnations, chrysanthemums, roses, tulips and lilies are cultivated to be sold.

So lush and wild is it, that 1200 bird and 359 animal species live here. The Great Himalayan National Park protects the rich flora and fauna of the main Himalayan range, and the Pin Valley National Park shelters animals like the snow leopard and Siberian ibex that enjoy the cold desert feel.

HIMACHALI HIGHS

India's highest polling booth is in Tashigang village in the Lahaul-Spiti district — up at 15, 256 ft!

Founded by the British in 1920, the Ice Skating Club in Shimla, is the largest open-air ice rink in India and South Asia's oldest natural ice rink.

apple ganesha

TRRRRIIIING!!

The school bell rang and Bhola rushed out of the class ahead of his classmates. He kept a steady pace as he climbed hilly paths lined with pine and cedar, and crossed terraced potato fields, stopping only when he reached a huge iron gate.

He climbed the horizontal bars till his head was above the gate and he could get a good view of what was on the other side. Above him was a sign in bold letters that read 'Royal Apple Orchard', and in front of him were rows and rows of trees laden with red, juicy apples.

Bhola gazed longingly at the apples. His school uniform — blue shorts and white shirt — had patches of dirt on it from the climb. His schoolbag dangled on the gate. His round, woollen cap, colourfully embroidered, was half off his head.

Kotgarh, where Bhola Prasad lived, was the apple heartland of Himachal Pradesh. This picturesque town near the capital, Shimla, had the silvery Sutlej flowing in the valley below and the snow-covered peaks of the faraway Himalayas towering above. There were many apple orchards in Kotgarh, but the Royal Apple Orchard was considered the best in the country as it had the reddest and juiciest apples.

Bhola had never tasted these delicious apples. Not many in Kotgarh had. That was because apples from this orchard were packed in big containers as soon as they were picked, and sent to different parts of the world. Bhola's parents would buy apples from the local market, but they were not half as scrumptious as the ones he was looking at now.

Every day, for the last few weeks, Bhola had followed the same routine of stopping by the orchard on his way back from school. Today, the watchman called out to him from inside: "Aree suniyo! Listen! Tomorrow is harvest day. You can come and watch if you like."

Bhola had made friends with the watchman, so he was not shooed off like the other boys.

The next day when Bhola reached the orchard, he found the gate open and a truck waiting outside. He entered and stood near the watchman's empty chair — the watchman was roaming among the trees, keeping a close watch, brandishing his stick. Apple harvesting was on in full swing. Ladders were placed against trees and men and women were picking the apples one by one. They would grip the apple gently with the palm of their hand, and then, in a twisting motion, separate it neatly from the branch. The apples were carefully placed in cane baskets. A group of workers packed the fruits from the baskets into wooden crates padded with hay, which were then loaded onto the truck.

Bhola was observing a man picking apples from a tree nearby when, suddenly, he saw a snake slithering near the man's feet.

"Watch out! Saanp! Snake!" he yelled.

The man turned around just in time, and drove the snake away. He looked at Bhola. "Hey little boy, come here," he called. "Thanks! You saved me. You can have an apple if you like."

Bhola's brown eyes lit up. The man's basket was full of juicy, red apples. But which one should he select? This one was bigger, but the next one looked redder. He had this one chance, and wanted the best. Unable to decide, Bhola closed his eyes and picked one. He placed it carefully in his school bag, and ran all the way home.

When he reached his house, he closed the door, took the apple out and was about to bite into it when— "Oh! What is this?" he thought.

In the evening Bhola's mother and father returned from the fields where they worked. They entered their small living room and were surprised by what they saw. On a wooden stool some flowers had been arranged, a lamp was lit, and Bhola was sitting cross-legged, hands joined in prayer. Seeing his parents, he said excitedly, "Ma, Papa! Dekho! See! Ganeshji!"

In between all the flowers sat an apple!

Bhola told his parents how he got the apple, and how just as he was about to eat it he saw that it looked exactly like Ganeshji. "Look, look!" urged Bhola earnestly. "It has this sprout, just like Ganeshji's trunk. And can you see the two dots for eyes?"

His parents didn't know what to say. They were amused but also touched by Bhola's devotion, even though it required them to stretch their own imagination. They smiled and nodded, and folded their hands in front of the apple so as not to hurt their son.

The next day Bhola's friends came over to see his Apple Ganesh for themselves and were awed by the resemblance of the apple to the god. Bhola told his friend the orchard watchman too, who came by and was suitably impressed.

On the third day, Bhola returned home from school to find a fancy red car parked outside his little house. "Who's visiting us?" he was wondering, when he saw a well dressed man wearing a big gold chain around his neck coming out of his house with his father.

"Thank you for coming, Sethji," his father told the man. He turned to Bhola and said, "Bhola beta, this is the owner of the Royal Apple Orchard. It seems his watchman told him about your Apple Ganeshji. Do namaste, beta."

Bhola folded his hands in greeting and quickly went inside. In front of his Ganeshji was a basket full of the reddest and juiciest apples — just the kind he had been waiting for, for a long, long time!

APPLE MANIA

Red, Royal, Richard, Baldwin, Jonathan, McIntosh Red, Yellow Newton, Ras–Pippin . . . If you are thinking 'names of foreigners', then Golden Delicious should alert you! These are all apples. Himachal, the apple state of India, grows 30 per cent of India's apples, which is 73 per cent of the fruits grown in the state.

It all started long ago in 1870 when Capt. A.A. Lee introduced apple growing in Kullu Valley. Then another Englishman, Alexander Coutts, who was tailor to Viceroy Lord Dufferin, started growing apples in his orchard called Hillock Head at Mashobra, Shimla. He brought 100 English apple varieties which seemed to like the soil and climate in hilly Himachal.

In 1919, about 80 km from Shimla, in Kotgarh, another foreigner started growing apples — an American, Samuel Evans Stokes. He used modern methods of farming and made apple cultivation what it is today. The apple variety he introduced was named American Delicious!

Stokes motivated farmers to improve their lives by growing apples. The elementary school he set up on his estate, trained children so that they would become good horticulturists. He was showing them the way out of poverty.

Digest this. On an average five lakh ton apples are produced each year.

Odisha

SWEETENING!

The rasgulla of Bengal may actually have had its beginnings in Puri. It is said that these soft spongy balls oozing light sugar syrup are as old as the famous Rath Yatra — and that they were made to feed and pacify goddess Lakshmi, who feels left out while her husband Jagannath is prayed to for 11 days!

The word 'juggernaut', loosely meaning a massive unstoppable force, comes from this gigantic chariot of Lord Jagannath, which is about 45 ft high and 35 ft square. It is pulled along with thick ropes by thousands of devotees. Once it rolls, it rolls. So if you don't move out, you know what can happen...

I COME FROM ODISHA

Fakir Mohan Senapati is considered the father of modern Odia literature and played a leading role in giving the Odia language a distinct identity.

International sand artist Sudarsan Pattnaik started sculpting images on sand as a child and has designed hundreds of amazingly intricate sculptures.

REWIND

The earliest settlers were hill tribes. Saora in the hills, and the Sahara and Sabar of the plains are still found almost all over Odisha.

Odisha is referred to as Utkala in the Mahabharata and in our national anthem. Also known as Udra or Odra Desa, it was Kalinga when the Maurya emperor Ashoka fought here in 261 BCE — a war that changed his life.

Under the Jaina emperor Kharavela (late 2nd century BCE) Kalinga extended south to parts of Tamil Nadu.

Harsha's empire in the 7th century CE included this region. The Ganga and Surya dynasties followed, under whom culture and architecture flourished — an example is the Konark Sun Temple.

The Sultanate of Bengal, the Mughals, the Marathas and the British all ruled over parts of Odisha.

TURTLE WALK

Gahirmatha beach is part of the Gahirmatha Marine Sanctuary, the largest nesting ground for Olive Ridley turtles in the world.

FLYING VISIT

In winter, Chilika Lake gets winged visitors from as far as the Caspian Sea, Lake Baikal, Aral Sea and other remote parts of Central Asia — about 160 migratory birds.

The endangered Irawaddy Dolphin also lives here.

ART 'WORK'

To make a pattachitra (meaning 'picture on cloth'), you have to first make tamarind seed glue and stick two sheets of cloth together. Then powder some clay stone, mix with the glue and coat the cloth. When it dries, polish the cloth smooth with a stone. Get the colours ready, by powdering stones and mixing them with the sap of the elephant apple tree. Now you can start painting — after making a brush out of keya root and mouse hair. That's how traditional art 'works', the natural way!

DIFFERENT STEPS

Odissi is said to be the oldest surviving dance form of India, dating to around the 2nd century BCE. An Udaygiri cave carving shows that it was performed in courts before it went into temples. It was reinvented later as gotipua nacha (done by little boys dressed as girls, called gotipuas) which influenced modern odissi. Guru Kelucharan Mohapatra, too, once learnt the gotipua dance.

Kalahandi's ghumura and Mayurbhanj chhau are folk dances that seem to have both tribal and martial origins. Elaborate masks are typical of Chhau.

WINDOW TO THE WORLD

If it's Tuesday, it must be Dukum!

That's certainly what seemed to be on everyone's mind as Binita's car passed hordes of villagers all headed that way — on foot, in vans, in buses, on bullock carts . . .

That's because Tuesday was haat day at Dukum. A typical village market scene greeted Binita and her grandfather there — colourful, noisy and vibrant. Temporary stalls made of bamboo poles and plastic sheets were set up on both sides of the road. Some had spread their wares on mats on the ground.

A Desia Kondh woman wearing three nose rings — on the left, right and middle of her nose — sold small bunches of arrowroot. A pony-tailed Dongria Kondh youth slung an axe over his shoulders as casually as Binita would her schoolbag. Older Kutia Kondh women, with geometrical tattoos on their faces, were selling fresh vegetables.

Binita's glasses were almost knocked off as she swerved out of the way of a woman carrying a pile of jackfruit stacked high on her head. The woman was dressed in what looked like a two-piece white robe. She had rows of beads around her neck and many hairpins in her hair.

For the Kondh tribals who live in the hills and plains of Odisha, it was a normal haat. For Binita it was the most extraordinary market she had ever seen — quite, quite different from anything in Bhubaneshwar!

The most exciting thing in her life so far had been the tablet PC she had coaxed and cajoled her parents into giving her for her birthday. Like most modern city children, she spent almost all her free time on the computer — playing games, browsing the internet or chatting online with friends.

And that is how she would have spent her month-long vacation, too, had it not been for her Jejebapa, her grandfather. He had to travel urgently to Bissam Cuttack to visit a friend who was unwell, and wanted Binita to come along. She loved him so she agreed, if a little reluctantly.

The bus journey had taken six hours. Binita alternated between playing games on her tablet and staring out of the window as sal and teak forests, turmeric and mustard fields, hills and hamlets passed them by.

Her grandfather's friend had been very pleased to see them and his family was warm and welcoming, but by evening Binita was bored stiff. There were no young people in the house, nothing to see in the town and the mobile network was too slow to use the internet. Sensing her discontent, Jejebapa had promised to take her to Dukum the next day, to see the weekly haat.

"Didn't I tell you it would be interesting? And everything is so fresh!" he now said, as he stopped to buy some jackfruit. He was trying to haggle with the seller, who was speaking in the Kuvi dialect used by the Kondhs.

This was going to take a while, Binita thought, and wandered off to see the other shops. She covered her nose as she passed the fish seller and hurried past the goats and fowls on sale. There were columns of aluminium vessels and stacks of handmade brooms. Binita breathed in the aroma of freshly ground spices, and then stopped to take a photo with her tablet of rows of colourful glass bangles.

Her eyes fell on the next stall, where a young tribal girl was selling metal bracelets, necklaces and chains. Binita was trying on a heavy bracelet, when she heard her grandfather call out for her. Realising he must be alarmed to find her gone, Binita slipped her hand out of the bracelet and ran to him.

"Bini, I told you to be with me," Jejebapa chided her. "Here, help me carry these." He had bought two jackfruits, one for their hosts and another to take back home with them. They loaded them in the car and started driving towards Bissam Cuttack.

"Where did you wander off?" he asked.

Binita babbled on about all she saw, how exciting it all was. "Then I was looking at some jewellery. I took a photo of these beautiful bangles — see!" said Binita, and reached for the tablet in her satchel.

It wasn't there!

"Oh, no! I forgot my tablet at the market!" she shrieked. "Turn back, quick! FAST!"

The next ten minutes were terrible. Binita was worried that by now her tablet would have been either stolen or damaged. What would she tell her parents?

She rushed through the market to the jewellery stall. A group of children had gathered there and, to her horror, were playing with her tablet!

"Eita moro! This is mine! Don't touch it!" she said, and snatched the tablet from them.

Back in the car, Binita checked the tablet for damages. She was surprised to see the screen with a photo of one of the kids. The children had clicked pictures, doodled in a paint app and played a game too.

"How did they do this? Surely this must be the first time they've even seen a computer!" wondered Binita.

They returned to Bhubaneswar the next day, but her thoughts were still with those tribal children. She looked at one of the drawings — the child had even figured out how to use different colours.

"Look at this!" she called out to her sister, Ankita. "If in about half an hour the six-seven-year-olds could do this much, then ... then ... you know what I am thinking ...!"

Next Tuesday, at 9 a.m., the Dukum market was just coming to life. It looked like it was going to be another regular haat day for the Kondhs. But it wasn't.

Binita, her sister Ankita, and two of her classmates, Debesh and Subrat, arrived at the marketplace with their own wares. Her grandfather's friend had helped to arrange for a makeshift stall. The children set up their laptops and tablets on the two tables in the stall and arranged cane chairs around them.

The locals were curiously watching them, though pretending to mind their own business. A few children, whom Binita had met the other day, stared from a distance.

"Tu computer khelibu ki? Do you want to play with the computer?" Binita called out in Odia to the children.

"That day you said not to touch it!" mumbled one boy.

"I am sorry. Today I want you to come and see it," replied Binita.

The boy and two of his friends came forward. Binita let them explore the computer, gently guiding them when they were stuck.

Seeing them enjoying themselves, more children came forward. They listened to rhymes and drew pictures.

While all this was happening, some grown-ups too slowly gathered around the stall. A few tribal men finally asked what they were doing there. They told the children that outsiders were not allowed to sell in their market.

"We are not selling anything. What we're doing is free!" asserted Binita.

The Kondhs were stumped. But hearing that it was free, a few men and women showed interest in their stall. The four youngsters had come prepared with downloaded content and CDs to engage everyone, from the youngest to the oldest.

Soon Ankita had several of them engrossed in videos of music and dance from other parts of Odisha and visuals of handmade jewellery.

Some watched an Odia news video that Subrat had downloaded in the morning. Others enjoyed the highlights of a cricket match with Binita.

Suddenly an authoritative voice boomed out something in Kuvi that the children couldn't fully understand. Immediately the tribals moved away from the stall and stood with their heads bowed.

It was obvious that the voice belonged to the head of the tribe, and it was also clear that he was very angry. He strode up to the foursome and told them, in Odia that the children could follow, not to teach nonsense to his tribe.

"How do we explain to him the importance of computers and the internet?" whispered Ankita desperately.

Binita responded boldly. "This is a window to the world!" she declared to the chief. The idea had just struck her and she thought it was a great comparison. "For so long the world has looked at all of you with curiosity. Don't you want to look at the world too?"

"Why don't you come and see for yourself? If you don't like it, we will go away!" pitched in Debesh.

A group of tribals gathered around their chief and seemed to discuss the matter. It must have seemed like a good idea, for the headman entered their stall.

Binita first showed him the laptop the younger children were still busy with, unconcerned with the chief's disapproval. They were having fun exploring on their own, and had even started learning the English alphabet and simple words. "So we can talk to the computer in its language," they had reasoned.

"Window to education!" said Binita, thinking what a marvellous heading this would make for a school project on computers!

Debesh and Subrat took him to the laptop the other groups had been using. They told him how those who had seen the news video had discussed the weather forecast and how it would affect their crops, and how some of them had jotted down new ideas for designing jewellery and other things.

"Window to information!" Binita came up with another heading.

A bigger group of slightly older children surrounded by young men and women had learnt about email. With Ankita's help they had even managed to send an email to the District Collector at Rayagada about the shortage of textbooks at their school. Ankita had to go near the highway to get a network, but finally the message was sent. "In our next email we can ask for a computer for our school," the children had said excitedly.

"Window to communication!" labelled Binita smartly.

"With good education, useful information and channels of communication, this computer will become a window to a better life!" added Subrat, catching on to Binita's theme.

"And it can be a window to participation too!" Ankita finished enthusiastically. "You can tell the world about yourself, about your lives. You can share your music, your talent in arts and crafts and your knowledge of nature."

The headman listened quietly. Then he came to a decision. He asked his people to get back to the computers, and himself watched a video about ancient tribes of the world!

Soon Binita and her group became a familiar sight at the weekly haat, where the tribals eagerly waited for a peek through the 'window' to the outside world.

MOUNTAINS OF RICHES

Odisha, with 62, has the highest number of tribes among Indian states. Many of them live on the mountains and depend on the forest for their needs. So closely are their lives intertwined with their environment and so conscious are they of protecting it, that they could teach 'modern' people a thing or two — for example, that development at any cost can be harmful for everyone in the long run, and that it is wrong to take land away from people who have always lived there.

Dongria Kondh tribals live in the Niyamgiri hills that have rich deposits of bauxite, which a company is intent on mining. If that happens, the Dongria Kondhs believe that the seat of their god Niyam Raja, their forests and rivers, will be destroyed. The Dongrias felt alone in their fight till news of their struggle spread — through the internet! Thousands of people then joined them in their protests, turning the court battle in their favour.

Uttarakhand

TESTING THE WATERS

Looking for adventure? You'll find it in the whitewater river rafting stretch of the Ganga from Kaudiyala to Rishikesh. Get ready for 12 major rapids over 36 km. With names like Cross Fire, Roller Coaster and Return to Sender, you know you're in for some thrills, spills and chills!

I COME FROM UTTARAKHAND

Girish Tiwari, 'Girda', was a poet who carried his message to the people during the movement to create Uttarakhand.

Children's writer Ruskin Bond has lived here for years and set many of his books among these mountains.

Bachendri Pal was the first Indian woman to climb Mount Everest.

REWIND

There has been human habitation in this region since prehistory. The Kols were one of the earliest known tribes to settle here, about 3,000 years ago.

There were two major kingdoms. Kumaon in the east was ruled first by the Kukindas from the 1st century BCE, and then by the Katyuris. Garhwal in the west was founded in the 1st century CE by the Rajput Panwars.

Ashokan edicts show that Buddhism was present here.

The Gurkhas of Nepal captured the region in the 19th century.

Uttarakhand was carved out of the Himalayan and neighbouring northwestern districts of Uttar Pradesh in 2000.

ICY COLD WOMB

Mountains cover 93% of Uttarakhand. Ganga and Yamuna, two of India's largest rivers are born up in its glaciers. This is the kind of place where sages loved to live! It is said, in fact, that the sage Ved Vyasa wrote the Mahabharata here.

DO NOT DISTURB!

The Jim Corbett National Park was set up in 1936, named after the hunter turned conservationist. India's first national park was also the first such in Asia, and the first sanctuary under Project Tiger. The Nanda Devi National Park shelters the endangered snow leopard and Himalayan musk deer. Along with the adjoining Valley of Flowers, it is a UNESCO World Heritage Site.

ECO WOMEN

In 1974, headed by Gaura Devi, a group of women in Reni village in Chamoli district prevented government contractors from felling trees by clinging to the trees. Their brave and non-violent act inspired many future environmental protests. This Chipko Movement was taken forward by others such as Sunderlal Bahuguna, who worked with local villages to protest against the destruction of mountains and forests.

SMALL IS BEAUTIFUL

In the mid-17th century CE, Suleiman Shikoh, a Mughal prince came to Garhwal with an artist and his son — his court painters — skilled in the Mughal miniature style. After some months, the prince left, but his painters were taken by the beauty of the region and stayed on. Their successors developed the style known as the Garhwal school of painting.

FLOORING THEM

Aipan is the Kumaoni art of drawing floor designs, much like alpona, rangoli and kolam elsewhere in India. The designs in rice paste can be geometric, or figures of gods and goddesses or motifs from nature. These can now be seen on shawls, wall hangings, photo frames, dupattas, even T-shirts. Tradition is trendy!

The Seven Snowmen

Catching her first glimpse of the snow-covered peaks of the Himalayas amongst the clouds, Jiya felt that the sky had parted to reveal the heavens, the home of the gods.

In the valley of Rishikesh at the foothills, the clear waters of the Ganga and the crisp mountain air made her feel close to the Himalayas. Now, at Ukhimath, the peaks were so near it was as if she had to just stretch out her hands to touch them . . . and grab a piece of the mountains for herself!

So when a plan was discussed for a day trek to Tungnath —'Lord of the Peaks', the highest of all the Shiva temples in the Himalayas — Jiya was thrilled!

But she was told only her father and two uncles would go, that she was too young.

The Malhotras were a large family on a pilgrimage to Uttarakhand, and this was the first time in her 11 years that Jiya would have a possible chance of seeing snow. She certainly wasn't going to let that go! Her mother, grandparents and aunts tried hard to dissuade her but Jiya was adamant.

Sensing the threat of the trek getting cancelled on account of this, her uncles convinced the others to let her come with them. The trek to Tungnath was a short one of about four kilometres, one of the easiest. And after all, there were three grown men to take care of her, so there was really no need to worry.

Before they left, Jiya's grandfather told her, "The mountains can be as dangerous as they are beautiful — remember that."

"I will!" said Jiya.

They had hired a vehicle and trekking gear, and set off at sunrise towards Chopta, the base camp. Jiya chattered non-stop and clicked photos all the way. As they drove higher, to Jiya's delight they saw an icing of snow on the meadows, hills, treetops and rooftops. The sun was shining as they neared Chopta, but snow lay thick on the road and it was clear they would have to do the last stretch of about half a kilometre on foot. Their trek had already begun.

Jiya lived in Mumbai where the weather only varied between hot, very hot and pleasant, and she had always craved to see snow. She held her breath now as her shoes sank into the soft, powdery snow and left a clear footprint.

They reached Chopta easily enough. A small hamlet, with hotels and shops catering mainly to tourists, the place looked deserted because it was the first week of November, almost the end of the season. The hotels were closed and houses boarded up. One or two small shops were open, however, and the trekkers went to one of them to have some hot tea and make some enquiries about the weather in Tungnath.

"This time winter has set in very early. The weather has been getting worse for the last few days. Last night there was heavy snowfall with more predicted for today," they were told. "Chopta is shutting down and so will the Tungnath temple."

Jiya's father, Hitesh, and his brothers, Akhilesh and Dinesh, discussed their options. No one wanted to turn back. The sun was shining brightly. There was no sign of the weather changing yet. If it did snow, it would probably be later in the day, by which time they would have returned.

Akhilesh had been to Tungnath just that summer, and was confident about the way. There was a clear stone paved path that led there, but blanketed as the whole place was with snow, he was cautious and told the others to tread carefully.

"Why do they say 'blanket of snow'? Blankets are supposed to keep you warm!" said Jiya.

"Look around you . . . doesn't it look like a soft fleece blanket spread by nature?" her father responded.

The trekkers walked in a line, with Akhilesh in front, followed by Hitesh, Jiya and Dinesh. Jiya found it easier to walk on the snow by stepping into the footprints her father and uncle left ahead of her.

As they climbed higher, the snow got deeper and deeper. Sometimes their legs got stuck in it and they needed the support of their trekking poles to haul themselves out. Their backpacks also slowed them down. There was a chilly wind, and though they were covered from head to toe in woollen caps, thermals, sweaters, weather-proof jackets, gloves and snow shoes, their teeth still chattered.

About 90 minutes into the trek, the sky darkened. The men grew anxious, but continued hoping the weather would hold. However, it began to snow lightly. After ten minutes, when they saw they were getting wet and slipping quite often, they stopped. There was a small roadside dhaba ahead, and they decided to take shelter there for a while. As they neared, they saw the owner about to shut shop.

"Bhaiya, one minute! Don't close!" Jiya's father called out.

The dhaba owner seemed shocked to see them. Clearly he was not expecting any customers today. "Can we come in? We are freezing," said Dinesh.

"We are going to Tungnath. We want to rest for some time," explained Akhilesh.

"Aree! Didn't anybody tell you that heavy snow is expected today?" said the man at last. "Chai peenai kya? Do you want some tea? You can come to my house, round the back. The dhaba is closed for the season."

The man introduced himself as Shivcharan. He had planned to keep his shop open for one more week, he told them, but because of the weather turning bad, everybody in the village had moved below to the valley much earlier this year. His wife and youngest son had gone already.

He and his other two children, Om and Alka, were packed and ready to leave that day, but had been held up by the snowfall.

Shivcharan's house was small, and had just two wooden benches, a small table and a cupboard in it. Two children — a little younger than Jiya — sat on one of the benches, gazing out of a large window, the only one in the house. When they saw the strangers, they quietly went to the kitchen to be with their father.

The Malhotras were glad they had carried an extra set of clothing in their backpacks. Changing into them, they hung up their damp clothes, caps and jackets to dry. They sat near the window, waiting for the snowfall to stop. But it only became heavier, and finally turned into a full-fledged snowstorm.

Shivcharan came in with lunch from the kitchen, which was common to the house and the dhaba. Hitesh asked if he could tell when the storm was likely to stop.

"It is difficult to tell, bhaiya. Hamar taem maa, in our time, there was once a snowstorm that lasted for a full fortnight," Shivcharan replied.

By evening, the storm had abated, but so had their hopes of returning to Ukhimath. It was pitch black outside. Hitesh and his brothers were uncomfortable about burdening themselves on Shivcharan. Where would they sleep? There were just those two benches. Besides, the house offered little protection from the storm. The windows rattled alarmingly and the cold wind seeped in from under the door, making them shiver. But where else could they go?

"Don't worry, you can stay in my house till it's safe to go. I have enough supplies to last for a week," Shivcharan told them, reading the look on their faces.

"Thanks, but we'll stay only for the night. Tomorrow morning we will be on our way," said Jiya's father.

"Theek cha! Fine! Now if you will come this way ..."

Shivcharan led them through his kitchen to a storeroom and opened a trapdoor in the floor that led to a basement below.

"My grandfather had built this not just for storing things, but also as a shelter during storms. It is made of stone and is really warm. Hamar taem maa, we have spent entire winters in this basement."

Jiya smiled. Shivcharan looked just a few years older than her own father, yet he spoke like he was an old man and these things happened a long, long time ago.

They climbed down into the basement. In the dim light of a dangling light bulb, Jiya noticed the children already fast asleep in a corner. She realised why the house above was so bare. Shivcharan had shifted everything to the basement – chairs, mattresses, a rickety couch. It was much warmer and cosier here, and the tired trekkers crashed out on the mattresses that lined the floor.

Early next morning, Shivcharan and Akhilesh stepped out to survey the situation. The snow had stopped. If the route was clear enough, the party would return to Chopta immediately.

They returned after almost an hour.

"There is good news and bad news," said Akhilesh. "The bad news is that there has been a mini-avalanche. The route back to Chopta is blocked by snow and debris."

His brothers stared in disbelief.

"What is the good news, Chacha?" asked Jiya.

"That we are alive! The scene is bad out there — it was a heavy storm," said Akhilesh.

"Haan, yes, that is true. By Tungnathji's grace, we are fine. And I am sure we will be on our way soon. The family must have lodged a complaint that we haven't returned when we were supposed to, and there must be people looking for us even as we speak," said Jiya's father reassuringly.

As the grown-ups continued their discussion about the weather, Jiya slowly entered the kitchen. Alka and Om were sitting quietly in a corner, absorbed in a game of snakes and ladders. "Can I also join you," asked Jiya shyly. She spent the rest of the day happily enough, playing and chatting with them.

The next morning, everyone was still in the basement when there was a loud, rumbling noise.

"An earthquake?" cried Dinesh.

"No, no," said Shivcharan. "Not earthquake, but–"

"Let's get out in the open," cut in Akhilesh. He opened the trapdoor and was out of there in a flash. The others followed him.

But the front door wouldn't open — the snow had blocked it from outside. Jiya meanwhile peered out of the window to see where the sound was coming from.

Shivcharan yanked open the window and jumped out. Om, Alka and Jiya jumped out too. And then, Jiya saw it — a helicopter, disappearing into the horizon!

They waved, shouted, screamed and ran till their feet got stuck in the snow . . . but it was too late.

For the first time in two days, the group felt a sense of despair. Till now they had been hopeful that they would be rescued soon, but they had missed their chance.

The four men decided to take turns waiting outside the house, in the hope of being noticed if the rescue helicopter came looking for them again. They would keep vigil from 7 a.m. to 7 p.m., and one of them would sleep upstairs in case the helicopter returned at night.

They had a difficult time. The sun refused to come out. It continued to snow, and they had to clear it from the front of the house every now and then, as it threatened to pile up till the window. And it was tough to keep a fire burning in the gale outdoors, robbing them of even a little warmth during their watch.

The men suffered from colds and stiff joints. Shivcharan, who had boasted about how he had spent many days out in the snow "in his time", was also under the weather.

The children tried to help them out in small ways by making tea, chopping vegetables, and tidying up the basement. Jiya had become good friends with the brother and sister. They swapped jokes, stories and even their secrets. Alka shared her comics and Jiya her chocolate bars.

It was Day 4. There was no further sign of any rescue team, and the road to Chopta was still blocked.

Jiya, Alka and Om were holed up inside the house and feeling very gloomy. The generator froze the previous evening, leaving them in darkness. Jiya had got very scared and longed for her mother's warm hug.

She badly wanted to be back with the rest of her family. She could see that Alka and Om wanted to be with their mother too.

"Why don't you children go out and play? It hasn't snowed since last night, and the sky looks clear this morning," said Jiya's father, coming in after his early morning watch and noticing how dull the children looked.

As Jiya stepped out of the house, she blinked in the light. She had been indoors for too long. Slowly, she took in the beauty of the surrounding mountains and peaks covered with snow — Chandrashila above her, and Chaukhamba, Kedarnath, Nanda Devi and Neelkanth in the distance. She was thrilled when she realised she was on a snow-clad mountain herself!

She remembered her grandfather's words and thought, "The mountains are as beautiful as they are dangerous."

Om and Alka brought out a few pebbles and stones and started playing with them. They called Jiya to join them.

"Why don't we play with the snow!" suggested Jiya.

Snow! White, pure, cold . . . there are many ways to describe it, but the best way to experience it is by holding it in your hands! Jiya wanted to make snowballs. Om and Alka showed her how to pack the snow as if making laddoos, then add more snow to make a big, round ball. But it was too cold to throw snowballs at each other. Om and Alka threw them up in the air instead and watched in delight as they crashed to the ground.

Jiya continued to pack the snow and made a rather big snowball.

"It will be very heavy! You won't be able to lift it from the ground!" cried Alka.

"I have an idea!" said Jiya. "Let's make a snowman!"

"What is a snowman?" asked the children.

Jiya was surprised they didn't know. She had seen children making snowmen on TV many times, and had thought that's what all children did when it snowed.

She rolled another big snowball and placed it on the first one, which crashed under the weight.

"Badhiya! Great! This is also fun," said Om.

"No, wait. This isn't what it is. I haven't got it right!" This time Jiya made the second ball slightly smaller than the one below, and placed it gently on top. It did not crash. Then she made a smaller one for the head. She used pebbles for eyes, a twig for the nose and shaped a smile with little stones.

"Our own snowman!" announced Jiya, and the children clapped and laughed.

Akhilesh and Dinesh came out to check on them. "A snowman! We never got a chance to make one as kids!" they exclaimed, and started to build their own, taking tips from the children.

Soon Shivcharan joined them. "So small?" he mocked at the two little snowmen the brothers had made. "Hamar taem maa we used to make big animals and such things out of snow. This…what is it called — snow-man? It looks easy!" And expertly, he began making a big snowman all by himself.

Not to be outdone, Jiya's uncles decided to join together and build a snowman bigger than Shivcharan's.

"Let's make the biggest snowman of all," said Jiya to Om and Alka, and they got busy packing and rolling big snowballs.

Meanwhile, finding the basement empty, Hitesh came out. After many days, he heard the sound of carefree laughter.

"Papa! Come, join us. You can build a snowman too. We will teach you," said Jiya excitedly.

She chattered on merrily with her father, giving instructions.

Soon, seven snowmen of different sizes stood in a semi-circle.

Akhilesh was ready with his camera.

"Wait!" said Jiya, and ran inside. She brought her red woollen cap and placed it on her snowman. "It is still damp from the snow, anyway, so it is better off on the snowman's head," she reasoned. "Anyway, our jackets have hoods and we have earmuffs and mufflers."

"In that case, get our caps also!" said her father.

Meanwhile, Om and Alka fetched two old and cracked buckets, and placed them on the other snowmen. Shivcharan brought his cane vegetable basket and placed it, upturned, on his snowman.

The snowmen looked smart in their different hats and ready for the photo session.

Time had flown by and they were all hungry as they trooped in for lunch. All these days, Shivcharan had been frugal in preparing food, as he didn't want to run out of supplies. Today, for a change, he served good portions of aloo matar, rotis, dal and rice. After the hearty lunch, they were all drowsy and decided to take a nap. Except for poor Dinesh, whose turn it was to be outdoors.

"Dinesh Chacha, why don't you also take a nap? I will keep watch," offered Jiya.

"That is very sweet of you, but you kids have been outside since morning ..." said Dinesh.

"I will be inside, sitting near the window."

"You will get bored."

"Of course not! I have the snowmen for company."

Jiya's father was the first to hear the whirring sound. He woke up the others. "Dinesh, wasn't it your turn to be outdoors," he said, as they all rushed out of the trapdoor.

Dinesh was about to reply when he saw Jiya curled up on the bench near the window, in deep sleep.

"Not again!" he thought, and joined the others as they ran out of the house. The helicopter was flying away from them!

Jiya woke up with a jolt and went outside. Everyone was staring at the empty sky.

"Hello!" said a stranger's voice behind her, and made her jump. She turned to where the snowmen were standing. "It can't be true!" she thought.

But between the snowmen were three people wearing the unmistakable uniform of the Indian Army.

The rescue team had an interesting story to tell. They had received two separate 'missing' complaints — one for three adults and a child, and another for one adult and two children. All of them were supposed to be in the area near Tungnath.

They had done an aerial survey two days ago, and not found anybody. This morning they were to do another check in this area. They were flying above the pristine white slopes when they noticed a few spots of colour. Flying a bit lower, they saw those were caps and hats. They counted seven in all. Could it be the seven missing people? They decided to check it out.

"Imagine our surprise when we saw seven snowmen standing there, instead of seven humans!" they said.

Shivcharan said, "Hamar taem maa ... I did not see anything like this!" and they all laughed.

The helicopter soon returned and they were airlifted with the help of cables. From inside the helicopter, Jiya looked down to catch a last glimpse of the snowmen, standing with their bright hats amidst the unending sheet of snow.

They melted on the next sunny day, but their photograph hangs in Jiya's room ... a piece of the mountains she can call her own!

AT HOME IN THE MOUNTAINS

Bachendri Pal climbed Mount Everest in 1984, when she was 30. Mountains were part of her life, for she had grown up among them in Nakuri, Uttarkashi. Once, when she was 12, she and her friends went on a picnic up a mountain that was 4000 m tall. When they reached the peak it was dark and they couldn't climb down. They remained there. No food, no shelter. It was frightening! But deep down, Bachendri knew the mountains would keep them safe. They made their way home the next morning.

Assam

UNDER COVER

The japi is perfect as a hat in summer and as an umbrella in the rains!
Made from bamboo, cane, or tokou paat (a large palm leaf), it gets its name
from jaap, which is a bundle of tokou leaves. Japis are offered as a sign of
respect during ceremonies. Placed near the front door, they say 'welcome'.

REWIND

Assam was once Kamarupa, ruled by the powerful Varman, Stalastamba and
Pala dynasties from the 4th to 12th centuries CE. Their kingdoms spread
over the Brahmaputra valley, north Bengal and north Bangladesh. Chinese
pilgrim Hiuen Tsang visited in the early 7th century, recording what he saw.

In the 13th century came Sukaphaa, a Tai from China. The Ahoms, descendants
of the Tai, ruled for nearly 600 years, mostly Upper Assam. The Tibeto-
Burmese Koch rulers controlled western Assam from the 16th century. The
Assamese are therefore a mix of races from China, Mongolia, Tibet, Thailand
and the northwest.

No Western power, not even the Mughals or British, could conquer Assam for
a long time. The locals used fierce guerilla tactics to keep them off. But when
the Burmese invaded Assam in the early 19th century, people fled to British-
ruled Bengal. The British then stepped in and slowly took control of the region.

I COME FROM ASSAM

Film-maker, singer, lyricist and political activist Dr Bhupen Hazarika
wrote and sang his first song at the age of 10. He went on to
introduce Assam's folk music to India.

Hindustani classical singer Parveen Sultana is from Nagaon.
She gave her first stage performance when she was 12.

RIVER FOLK

During the heavy monsoon rains, the streams that join the Brahmaputra river bring down silt from the hills. This piles up as sandbanks to become chars or river islands. Majuli, is the world's second largest. People who live on chars move around on bhoors, rafts made of banana stem.

COLOURS OF SILK

Assam is a leading silk producer of the country — the golden muga, white paat and eri are found only here. Eri worms feed on castor leaves, paat worms on mulberry leaves. Muga worms prefer som and sualu leaves. And Sualkuchi is the village that is the centre of the silk industry.

GO BAMBOO!

Muli, Dalu, Khang, Pecha...
These are just four of more than 30 species of bamboo that grow in Assam. Bamboo is used for a whole lot of things, from construction to furniture, tools, toys, baskets and umbrella handles. One of the fastest growing plants on earth, it is also used for medicines. And its shoots make declicious soups and curries!

TEA TIME STORY

Robert Bruce, a Scotsman, found that the Shingpo tribe ate the leaves of a wild plant with garlic and also used the leaves to brew a hot drink — tea! A few years later, with their help the British laid out tea plantations. In 1838, London got its first bags of Assam tea. Assam produces about 51% of India's and 16% of the world's tea.

FUELLED

An oil well was mechanically drilled in Makum as far back as 1867! Upper Assam still has good reserves of petroleum, natural gas and coal. The Digboi Refinery (1901) is the oldest working oil refinery in the world.

the piper of manas

"Doomsday! This is how the world will–"

The sentence hung mid-air as a bolt of lightning ripped the sky in half, illuminating the desolate, submerged landscape.

In that fraction of a second, Dr Subhendu Phukan saw the silhouette of something on the branch of a tree, barely above water level. He couldn't believe his eyes!

"Stop talking nonsense and take the boat near that tree!" he shouted to his mate in the rescue boat.

Sure enough, wedged dangerously between the tree trunk and a branch was a baby rhinoceros!

The sound of thunder shook the earth and the furious tide almost capsized their small boat. His colleague steadied the boat as Dr Phukan reached out to the scared animal, using all his strength to heave the calf off the tree.

Just then, the branch gave way and fell with a big splash into the water. If they had been a minute late, the baby would have been washed away in the floods. As big blobs of rain began to fall again, the doctor wrapped the calf in his raincoat, and slowly steered the boat back to safety.

The baby rhinoceros was lucky. Every monsoon, the mighty Brahmaputra swells and submerges Kaziranga National Park that lies in its flood plains. This year, the deluge was more severe because of the relentless heavy rains. Most of Kaziranga was under water, and hundreds of animals had been washed away trying to escape to higher land. Among them could possibly have been the mother of this rhino calf.

Dr Phukan, a veterinarian, had come from Assam's other well known national park, Manas, to volunteer in the rescue operations. Back at the camp, he attended to the rhino calf. The injuries were not grave, but the calf needed close monitoring for the next 48 hours. Coming to a decision, Dr Phukan sought the necessary permissions and took the rhino with him to Manas.

His two children, Arnab and Radhika, came running out when their father got home, and squealed delightedly to see the calf. Arnab was ten and Radhika was five years old. They had grown up surrounded by animals, and were very comfortable with them.

The baby rhino looked at them with his little button eyes.

"Iman morom lage — he's so cute! Look at his pointed ears!" said Radhika.

"And this little bump on his nose . . ." added Arnab.

"That's where the horn will grow," their father told them. "He is, after all, a Great Indian One-horned Rhinoceros."

Dr Phukan took the calf to the stabilisation centre, where he was to be monitored. He returned home in the evening, looking very worried.

"What is the matter, Deuta?" Arnab asked him. "Is it something about the rhino?"

"No, no, nothing! He needs time to adjust, that's all," replied his father.

But Dr Phukan was actually very worried about the rhino. The baby was traumatised. He was just a few weeks old, and probably missed his mother. He had to be fed every three hours, but giving him a bottle of milk had been a struggle. He had not stirred from his place the whole day, despite their best efforts to get him up and about. The doctor knew that if this went on, the baby would not survive too long.

The next day, after school, Arnab and Radhika went off to see the rhino calf. He was lying down in a corner of the open enclosure. They were told that their father was out on work but expected back soon. Since he had forbidden the children from ever approaching wild animals on their own, they moved a little away to wait for him.

Arnab was learning to play the flute and always carried it with him. He started to play a new tune he had learnt in music class that day. He played well — each note in place, the tone bright, the pitches rising. The lively folk tune got Radhika dancing and twirling around her brother.

Arnab had closed his eyes and was concentrating on the music when he felt Radhika clutch his arm and shake him. He stopped playing and opened his eyes.

The baby rhino was standing just a few feet away from them!

Equally surprised, the rhino moved back a few paces, ready to go back to its corner.

"Play again! Play again!" whispered Radhika.

Arnab put the flute to his lips and played the same tune again. The calf slowly came near them, bobbing his head and squealing as if enjoying the music. Radhika stroked the rhino's back.

Dr Phukan had returned a few minutes earlier, and was watching the scene in amazement. It was true that animals responded to music. Not just cats and dogs, but even big animals like horses cantered to music, and elephants could even play certain instruments. But he was sure there had been no previous study about the effect of music on rhinoceroses. Then again, it was possible that they could respond to music as a rhino's hearing is quite sharp and they make a variety of high and low pitched sounds themselves. Or could it be that this particular rhino calf was special?

"Deuta!" cried Radhika, noticing her father. "You know what happened just now? Arnab was playing his flute and I was dancing and the baby rhino came near us! Isn't it great? Just like the Pied Piper story!"

"It is more fantastic than the story. After all, rhinos are much bigger than mice," replied the dazed doctor.

That was when the children decided to name the calf Baahi, which meant 'bamboo flute' in Assamese.

Dr Phukan realised there was now a way to get Baahi back to normal. Arnab and Radhika were only too excited to help. Arnab played the flute for Baahi every day. Radhika helped to feed the calf. Soon the baby rhino came running to Arnab every time he heard the flute and, like Radhika, went round and round him, as if dancing to the tune.

The shrill sound of the phone ringing woke up the Phukan household at 4 a.m. on a Sunday morning. After a brief conversation on the phone, Dr Phukan hurriedly gathered his things to leave.

"What is the matter? Where are you going?" his wife asked.

The doctor looked at the sleepy faces of Arnab and Radhika and hesitated. Then he said, "It's Baahi — he is missing!"

The children insisted on going with their father. The last time they had seen Baahi was about five months ago. In the last three years, Baahi had grown along with the children. He now weighed about 1000 kilos, had armour-like skin folds and a small, pointy horn. For the children, though, he was the same little baby who came running to them and danced with them. He was their pet, their friend.

But rhinoceroses are wild animals and Baahi had to be released back in the wild. He had to go to a rhino boma — a place that provides safety from predators while young rhinos get acclimatised to the new environment. There was one such temporary enclosure in the Banasbari range within Manas, and that's where Baahi was to be taken. Arnab and Radhika had bid their friend a tearful goodbye and were not allowed to have contact with him after that.

On reaching the Banasbari boma now, the children and their father at once saw what had happened. A section of the fence was broken, trampled upon by a herd of wild elephants who had rambled that way in the dead of the night. There was enough of a gap for Baahi to wander off into the wild unknown.

Just then, the ranger of the park arrived in his jeep. He gave a brisk nod to the doctor.

"Good, good, you have come! We need you on standby, doctor. Have you got all the medical equipment?"

"Of course," said Dr Phukan. "But wasn't the rhino radio-collared? Why is it taking so much time to trace him?"

"He was, he was. But, well, it is not working. We can't trace him."

"Sir, then how will Baahi be found?" questioned Arnab.

"Who's Baahi? Oh . . . I see, your rhino friend? Well, we are doing what we can. All the forest camps are on high alert. I have just come from the village — there have been no rhino sightings. It is more likely, highly likely, that the rhino is in the park itself. He is sure to be sighted by our patrol guards."

"Why don't you send a helicopter?" said Radhika.

"Helicopter!" roared the ranger. "Where will I get a helicopter? I wish I had one! Yes, I wish I had one."

It was almost noon. The surveillance jeeps had not been able to find the rhino. The doctor and his children were waiting in the ranger's office.

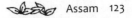

He had just got off the phone with someone from his head office. "I have just been informed it could take two or three days for them to send the latest equipment needed to trace the rhino," he groaned.

Arnab stood up and said, "Sir, please let us help you find Baahi."

The ranger stared at him. "You are telling me that you — YOU — can find him when we can't?"

"No, Baahi will find us!" replied Arnab.

The ranger didn't know what to think. The boy seemed to mean it, but the idea was outrageous! Not wanting to hurt the children, he merely said it would be against park regulations so he couldn't allow it.

Dr Phukan, too, said, "We will have to wait and watch."

"If Arnab or I were lost would you still wait and watch, Deuta?" said a teary Radhika.

"Baahi is only three years old and not used to the wild. He needs our help," pleaded Arnab.

Dr Phukan was well aware of the dangers Baahi could face from poachers and tigers. "Ah! Mur lora suali, my children, I am with you!" he said, getting emotional. He convinced the ranger to give it a try, agreeing to take full responsibility for the plan.

They set out in the ranger's jeep, north from Banasbari, and after about a kilometre made their first stop. Arnab took out his flute and started to play Baahi's favourite tune. It sounded like the call of a beautiful bird and echoed in the silence of the jungle. The doctor and Radhika scanned the surroundings.

A pygmy hog appeared out of the bushes. A few birds started calling out their own tunes. But there was no sign of a rhino.

"In which direction do you want to go now?" asked the ranger.

To the west they could see the Manas river, which flowed down from Bhutan, and the surrounding marshes and riverine forests. To the east were grasslands. And if they were to continue straight along the river bank, they would reach the dense tropical forests of Mothanguri, near the Indo-Bhutan border.

They decided to go towards the grasslands, as it was the favoured habitat of rhinoceroses. Their jeep was diverted from the road to a rough track. Every kilometre or so they stopped, and Arnab played the tune again and again. But there was not an animal in sight. The grass grew so tall all around, it could have even hidden an elephant.

They were soon deep in the Bhuyanpara range, the hunting ground of tigers. If Baahi was here, he could be in real danger!

The ranger was beginning to worry about the safety of the children. What if a tiger took offence to the music? His own ears were ringing after hearing the same tune over and over again. He considered the whole experiment a waste and insisted they turn back.

But Arnab only took in a deep breath and played the tune once more.

This time there was some movement in the grass a little way away. Was it the wind? Or could it be a tiger?

It was a rhinoceros! And it was charging towards them at full speed!

The ranger aimed the tranquiliser gun but the doctor held the muzzle, signalling him to wait.

The rhinoceros was very near the jeep and in a second there would be a massive collision. But then, the animal came to a sudden halt, barely two feet away, and started circling the jeep.

It was a fantastic sight! The ranger's jaw dropped, the doctor clapped his hands, Radhika jumped up and down with joy, the piper of Manas played his tune, and Baahi danced round and round in circles.

RHINO RESCUE

There are only about 2000 Great Indian One-horned rhinos left in the wild. The Kaziranga and Manas National Parks are their safe havens. Though huge, rhinos are excellent swimmers. But that's not much help during the monsoons when Kaziranga gets flooded. If they leave the park in search for higher ground, they are at risk from poachers. The Centre for Wildlife Rehabilitation and Conservation (CWRC) rescues displaced rhino calves.

Punjab

WHEAT TREATS

Roti, paratha, naan, kulcha... With a dollop of butter, Punjab's flavourful hot breads are unmatched! The five rivers — Beas, Chenab, Sutlej, Ravi and Jhelum — not only give the state its name 'punj-ab', the 'land of five rivers', they make the soil very rich. That's why Punjab grows the most wheat in India.

I COME FROM PUNJAB

Wing Commander Rakesh Sharma became the first Indian to go into space in 1984.

Kiran Bedi joined the Indian Police Service (IPS) in 1972 and became its first female officer.

● Hockey player Balbir Singh (Sr) was part of three Olympic gold medal winning teams, and has the record for most goals scored by an individual in an Olympic men's hockey final.

FOOD FOR THE SOUL

Every day, volunteers from different faiths and communities cook, clean and serve a wholesome vegetarian lunch at the Guru ka Langar, the community kitchen at Amritsar's Golden Temple. Amar Das, the third Sikh guru, started the practice of eating as equals in the 16th century. It lives on. Around 80,000 eat on weekdays and twice as many on weekends — and lunch is on the house!

VILLAGE VIGOUR

Over three days in February, the strength, skill and stamina of 4000 men and women, young and old, are tested in quirky ways at the Kila Raipur Sports Festival — India's Rural Olympics. They race tractors, carry bicycles with their teeth, play tug of war and race astride two galloping horses! The bullock cart race is the highlight.

◀◀ REWIND

The 5000-year-old Indus Valley Civilisation spread along the Indus river, from Afghanistan, through Pakistan, into Punjab, and on to Gujarat.

As the gateway from the west to India's fertile plains, the region was frequently under attack. Apart from the Greeks led by Alexander, it was invaded by the Persians, Bactrians, Scythians, Arabs, Turks and Afghans, who all left behind a cultural impact.

Parts of Punjab were in the empires of the Mahajanapadas, Mauryas, Kushans and Guptas, then of the Delhi Sultans, Mughals, Marathas and the British.

Guru Nanak Dev founded the Sikh religion in the 15th century. Maharaja Ranjit Singh started the Sikh Empire in 1799 that flourished for 50 years.

In the Partition of 1947 the original state of Punjab was split into two — the west went to Pakistan, the east to India. In 1966, Punjab was divided again, with chunks taken to create Haryana and Himachal Pradesh.

FLOWERY TROUSSEAU

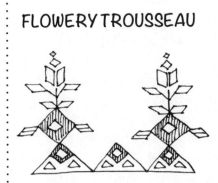

A Punjabi bride gets a special gift from her mother — phulkari, 'floral embroidery', worked on for years. The designs are aptly called bagh, 'garden'. Warm yellows, green and amber silk threads are stitched on reds or rusts. The stitches are perfect, for one mistake can upset the sequence. So perfect, that a wrong stitch is deliberately inserted to ward off the evil eye!

A GRAND OLD ROAD

The 2500 km Grand Trunk Road starts from Peshawar in Pakistan, cuts through Amritsar, Jalandhar and Ludhiana in Punjab, and goes down the Gangetic plain to end at Chittagong in Bangladesh.

It follows the ancient route that connected the east and west of the Indian subcontinent for over 2000 years. Once Uttarapath, then Sadak-e-Azam, it is now India's National Highway 1 (NH1) from Punjab to Delhi, and NH2 from there eastward.

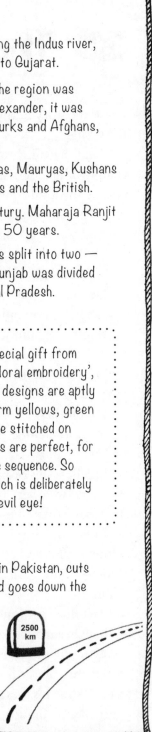

2500 km

The Wrestling Match

This is the story of the strongest boy in Punjab — Tiny Singh ... er ... Tejbir Singh.

Tejbir lived in a small village in the Amritsar district. He belonged to a family of wrestlers. His grandfather, father and uncles were trained in akharas, the local centres. They had fought kushtis, and won medals and fame. They were all tall, strong and well built men.

And was Tejbir the strongest and most famous of them all?

NO!

Tejbir was short and thin and ... well, tiny!

He looked even tinier in front of his two brothers Balbir and Satbir, though they were only a few years older than him.

Bunty and Sunny, as his brothers were called at home, would gulp down a jug of lassi and polish off a stack of aloo parathas topped with melting butter. Tiny barely managed to get through one glass of lassi and two parathas.

His brothers exercised every morning with wooden maces and dumbbells. Fetching the equipment for his brothers was workout enough for Tiny.

In school, his brothers were the stars of the wrestling and hockey teams, and were very popular. Tiny was also in the team, but as the mascot! He was the only one who could fit into the shabby lion costume.

Bunty and Sunny teased him endlessly about it. "Khodeya sher da costume te nikklya chooha. Dug into the lion's costume and found a mouse — Tiny!" All the other children in school also often made fun of him.

And this Tiny Singh became the strongest boy of Punjab!

It all began when, one day, Bunty and Sunny gifted a teeny-tiny mouse to their brother as a joke. Tiny was very angry and got into a fight with them. Later, when he had cooled down, he felt something soft and furry tickling his toes.

It was the mouse.

Tiny picked it up and held it on his palm. It was much smaller than any mouse he had seen. Tiny knew how the little fellow must be feeling and decided to keep it as his pet.

Chottu the mouse soon became his constant companion. Tiny had the last laugh when Chottu escaped from his cage one day, and nibbled through his brothers' notebooks. When Bunty and Sunny turned up in class with "mouse ate our homework" excuse, it only got them into bigger trouble!

But what is a mouse doing in a story about the strongest boy in Punjab? Well, you'll see!

It was April, the harvesting season for the winter rabi crop that now stood tall in the fields. Golden-brown stalks of wheat swayed in the sunshine.

It was a busy time for Tiny's father who managed their ancestral farm. The brothers often accompanied their father on his tractor and helped with the odd jobs at the farm. A dozen workers cut the wheat stalks and bundled them into large stacks. A threshing machine was used to separate the grain from the chaff and stem. The wheat was ready to be loaded onto trucks and hauled to a mandi to be sold.

And then it was time to celebrate Baisakhi, the harvest festival!

In the morning, Tiny went to the gurudwara along with his brothers, parents and grandfather. They wore new clothes (Tiny looking shiny in his new kurta-pajama and turban) and carried a small offering from the harvest.

Baisakhi is also an important religious festival, as it was on a Baisakhi day, that Guru Gobind Singh, the tenth Sikh guru, founded the order of the Khalsa. So Tiny's family attended the special prayer meet, after which delicious kara prasad — sweet halwa, dripping with ghee — was distributed.

When the family returned home in the afternoon after a sumptuous langar, the community lunch, they found Rajinder, Tiny's uncle, waiting for them. For the last two years, he had been training to be a professional wrestler in a famous akhara in Ludhiana. In addition to rippling muscles, he was also full of beans — not of the rajma bean variety, of course! He was lively, energetic and happy. In short, he was a favourite uncle.

"Oye Raj, it's great to see you! I tried calling you so many times, why don't you answer your cell phone?" said Tiny's father.

"Sorry, Praji, my cell is with Dhanno ... the akhara's buffalo."

"What! Your buffalo uses a cell phone?" exclaimed Bunty and Sunny.

"Arrey, it so happened that it was my turn to feed Dhanno, when my mobile slipped and fell into her fodder," sighed Rajinder. "Bas, that was the end ..."

"Of Dhanno?"

"Nahi yaar, no! Of my mobile. Dhanno swallowed it whole!"

It turned out that Rajinder was on his way to participate in the dangal, the wrestling competition, at the Baisakhi fair in a nearby village. He invited all of them to come, but there was still so much work to be done in the fields that only the children could go along. Early next morning, the boys set off with their uncle for the fair.

The Baisakhi fair was crowded, with people haggling at the numerous stalls selling everything from household items to toys and  trinkets. The sound of nagada drums was interspersed with the screams of children on fast rides. The warm aroma from food stalls made everyone hungry.

Rajinder led the children straight to the other side of the field, where a wrestling pit was being readied. Turmeric and oil were added to the mud — to keep it moist and give it antiseptic properties, Rajinder told the boys. Rows of tents were pitched nearby for the competitors. They found their tent and dumped their bags inside.

"You know what is so special about this year's dangal? The famous wrestler Moochad Lal Pehelwan has come to participate in it!" said Rajinder, pointing to the tent next to theirs.

A six-foot-four-inch tall, broad shouldered man wearing a dhoti was standing near the entrance. His well oiled muscular body glistened in the sun. His head was completely shaven. But what captivated Tiny was his thick moustache, which sloped downwards and rose up in big curls, covering his cheeks. Moochad was feared by his opponents as much for his impressive moustache as for his giant size. He had won many tournaments and called himself the strongest man in Punjab.

"Oye, don't worry, I don't have to fight him. We are not in the same category," said Rajinder, trying to soothe his visibly awestruck and nervous nephews.

Having seen enough of the star of the show, Tiny and his brothers went to see the fair's other attractions. They whirled in merry-go-rounds, rocked in a boat-shaped swing, rolled in the giant wheel, and if it wasn't dizzying enough, went for another turn.

They stuffed themselves with tandoori chicken, sweets and ice cream. They shot balloons with an air rifle, knocked down pyramids of tumblers, and threw rings at packets of biscuits and small gifts arranged on a table.

In the afternoon, they went to watch their uncle wrestle and cheered as he won the bout.

But the most watched matches were those with Moochad Lal Pehelwan. He swept all the matches in the preliminary rounds, and with each win became more and more arrogant. He would twirl his moustache and laugh at his fallen opponent. Tiny didn't like him at all.

Bunty and Sunny also participated in the Juniors' category. They gloated about it in front of Tiny.

"Too bad, Tiny, there is no Babies' category for you to take part in," teased Bunty.

"Our little Tiny would have lost even there," sneered Sunny.

Tiny was still seething with anger when Rajinder entered with a wrestler friend.

"Vicky, these are my three nephews," he said.

"Kitthe? Where? I can see only two and a half," joked the friend. Sunny and Bunty roared with laughter, but for Tiny it was like rubbing salt on his wounds.

He went to bed feeling miserable.

The next morning he woke up with a start. It was still very early and his brothers were asleep.

He was about to go back to sleep when he realised that he had forgotten to feed Chottu last night. Unknown to the others he had brought his mouse with him, concealed in a shoebox. Tiny went to check on him. But the box was open, and the mouse was missing!

Tiny hurried outside. A few people were moving about, busy with their morning chores. Many were still sprawled out on charpais outside their tents. The rides stood still and stalls were yet to open for the day. The field seemed much bigger now than yesterday amidst the crowds.

Where was he going to look for his teeny-tiny mouse?

Just then he heard some voices from the next tent. Maybe he should check there first, he thought and peeped into the tent of Moochad Lal Pehelwan. The tent was much bigger than Tiny's and had a partition at one end. The voice was coming from behind it.

"Everyone will laugh at me!" a furious Moochad Lal was saying.

"Koi gal nahi, don't worry," said another man, with a little panic in his voice.

"What do you mean, don't worry! How can I fight now? My moustache was my identity. How will I face the people?" said Moochad emerging from behind the partition.

Tiny was shocked! The burly pehelwan's curling moustache was gone! All that remained was just a short fuzz under the nose. Now, Hitler was probably the only man who could look terrifying with a small moustache — the rest end up looking like Charlie Chaplin.

Tiny had to now stuff his fist into his mouth to stifle his laughter. He almost choked! Just then he felt a familiar tickle on his toe — it was his mouse! A thought suddenly hit Tiny. "Chottu, is this your mischief? Did you do that to Moochad?" he chuckled, as he put the mouse in his pocket and quickly returned to his tent.

If he hadn't still been angry with his brothers, he would have probably told them what he had seen. Instead he followed them silently, determined to enjoy the last day of the fair. After watching some vigorous bhangra performances, acrobats jumping through loops and a magician perform tricks, Tiny bought a wooden engine for himself and sweets to take home.

The final wrestling matches were scheduled for the afternoon. Rajinder won the trophy in the lightweight category, to the delight of his nephews.

The finale of the tournament was the bout between Moochad Lal and his opponent.

A big crowd had gathered by then, and Tiny had to squeeze his way to the front. He wondered if Moochad would really come for the fight after what had happened in the morning. But the pehelwan did appear, and he seemed to have regained not only his confidence but also his famous moustache!

Moochad Lal pinned down his opponent in no time and the crowd broke into applause. Gloating in the admiration, Moochad threw open a challenge to the audience: "Is there anyone here strong enough to fight me? Come and face me — come on!"

There was a lot of murmuring but, unsurprisingly, no one seemed willing to take him on.

"All scared? Can't fight me? Ha! I am the strongest in Punjab!" he bragged.

Suddenly Tiny jumped into the ring. "I will challenge you!" he yelled at the top of his voice. It took some time for Moochad and the crowd to spot the challenger. Laughter broke out when they saw little Tiny in the middle of the pit.

"Scoot, kid, this is not your school playground," guffawed Moochad.

"He must have got pushed in by mistake. Come back, puttar," said an elderly man.

But Tiny was not there by mistake. He intended to fight and stood squarely facing Moochad Lal.

While Moochad was still laughing, Tiny gave a war cry, took a run up, and using Moochad's bulging arms for support, jumped onto him.

Half squatting on his chest, with a foot on each shoulder, Tiny held on to Moochad's shiny head. Tiny's shirt was now blocking the pehelwan's face and Tiny's head was just above Moochad's head.

Moochad was annoyed. "Get down, or I will throw you down," he boomed.

"In a minute," replied Tiny.

He let go of Moochad's head and grabbed the two ends of his moustache. Their eyes met briefly, and Tiny saw a fleeting flash of fear in Moochad's. Holding tightly onto the bushy moustache, Tiny pushed both his legs hard into Moochad's shoulders, and using them as a springboard, jumped backwards and fell to the ground.

In his hands was Moochad's famous moustache. He held it up like a trophy.

The crowd was stunned. It was as if Tiny had pulled the stripes off an angry tiger, the horn off a charging rhinoceros, the teeth off a hungry crocodile, the ... well, you get the idea.

Unable to believe what had happened in the last few seconds, Moochad felt his face in horror. It was like the fields after Baisakhi, absolutely bare!

The crowd, having recovered from the drama, started jeering and laughing.

For a moment Moochad seemed to be wondering what to do next. Then, unable to bear the embarrassment, he ran out, his hand covering his face.

The referee had no other option but to declare Tiny the winner.

The crowd went crazy. They had not seen this much excitement since the day, five years ago, when a bull had wandered into the fair and dozed off in the cool mud-pit. All the pehelwans could not budge him an inch. The bull had finally given up when a wrestler pulled his tail, but not before chasing the offender four times around the ground.

But today's event had clearly topped the charts.

Bunty and Sunny broke away from the cheering crowd, ran into the pit and lifted Tiny on their shoulders.

"This is Tejbir Singh and he just defeated Moochad Lal," they shouted. "That makes him the strongest boy in Punjab!"

Shouts of "Bhai wah!" and "Punjab da sher!" rang all around. Tiny was the new hero!

Rajinder, though, was a little upset. On the way back, when Bunty and Sunny were dozing, he questioned Tiny. "Puttar, why did you do such madness? I had only gone away for a little time — if I had been there, I would not have allowed you to take such a risk! You could have got hurt, you know."

"Don't worry-shurry, Chacha, nothing would have happened to me," said Tiny, and told him all about the missing mouse and missing moustache. "So when I saw Moochad with his moustache in the pit, I guessed that—"

"Wait! Let me guess. You thought that Moochad had some magic hair-growing potion?"

"Chacha!"

"Ah yes, you guessed that the person you saw in the morning was his twin!"

"Nooooo, Chacha. I guessed he was wearing a fake moustache."

"Yes, yes, that would have been my next guess . . ."

"Anyway, I knew if I could only pull them out, he would be too embarrassed to fight. So when he threw the challenge, I took the chance. Did I do something wrong? Was it cheating?"

"Wrestling is not only about physical strength, puttar. You also need to use your brains, which you did."

And so, the strongest boy in Punjab came home to a hero's welcome.

All the people in his village showered him with gifts and praises. Tiny shared all the edible goodies with Chottu, whose mischief had led to his victory.

Tiny's brothers were in awe of him and nobody at school teased him about being small any more.

But Tiny didn't mind being tiny any more, for he knew now that a tiny mouse could also bring a mighty lion to its knees.

MAKING THE MOVE

Two great pehelwans in the 1900s were Imam Baksh and his brother, Ghulam Muhammad. Of 5000 wrestling bouts, Ghulam, the 'Great Gama', lost just one! Punjab's traditional sport, pehelwani or kushti, combines the principles of Persian wrestling, a local form called mal-yudh and yoga. In India, the champion gets the title Rustum-i-Hind. Rustum was a legendary Persian warrior-king, the greatest pehelwan of his time. Pehelwans belong to akharas or gyms, of which there are about 300 in Punjab.

Little Indians: Stories from across the country (English)

ISBN 978-93-5046-354-3
© *text* Deepika Murthy
© *illustrations* Tulika Publishers
First published in India, 2013
Reprinted in 2015, 2019

Published by
Tulika Publishers, 305 Manickam Avenue, TTK Road, Alwarpet, Chennai 600 018, India
email reachus@tulikabooks.com *website* www.tulikabooks.com

Printed and bound by
Manipal Technologies Limited, Manipal